Laurie Critchley has worked
and has produced documen
currently employed as a co
Women's Press in London. *
Green: Women Writing on G
1996), co-editor of *Feast! W*
Women's Press, 1996), and
young adult series, Livewire.

Helen Windrath is senior commissioning editor and rights
manager at The Women's Press. Prior to this she worked
for Commonword, a north-west community publisher, based
in Manchester. She also edited *The Women's Press Book
of New Myth and Magic* (The Women's Press, 1993) and
Reader, I Murdered Him, Too (The Women's Press, 1995).
She lives in London.

Also edited by Laurie Critchley and Helen Windrath from The Women's Press:

The Women's Press Book of New Myth and Magic (1993) ed Helen Windrath

Reader, I Murdered Him, Too (1995) ed Helen Windrath

A Glimpse of Green: Women Writing on Gardens (1996) ed Laurie Critchley

Feast! Women Write About Food (1996) eds Laurie Critchley and Helen Windrath

Something to Savour

Food For Thought From Women Writers

Laurie Critchley and Helen Windrath, editors

First published by The Women's Press Ltd, 1996
A member of the Namara Group
34 Great Sutton Street, London EC1V ODX

British Library Cataloguing-in-Publication Data
A catalogue record for this book is available from the British
Library

ISBN 0 7043 4507 2

Phototypeset in 11 on 13pt Bembo by Intype London Ltd
Printed and bound in Great Britain by BPC Paperbacks Ltd

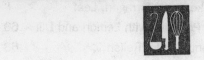

CONTENTS

INTRODUCTION

Put two editors in adjoining offices, add a shared interest in food, leave to simmer for several months and the result is *Something to Savour* – a collection of recipes and recollections from leading women writers around the world.

Recognising that our own enjoyment of food was often linked to the wider pleasures of conversation, community and creativity, we invited some of our favourite writers to share their own associations with food, through the contribution of a recipe together with the 'story' behind it. We were, we have to confess, a little nervous! As women extend their sphere of influence far beyond the kitchen, food and cooking may well be something many women do not wish to dwell on, with good reason. Happily, the response was overwhelming and women were intrigued and stimulated by the prospect of putting on paper some of their thoughts on the subject. Whether cooking for themselves, feeding others or being cooked for, the great majority of those we approached had a recipe and 'reason' they were happy to share.

From the taste of mother's love to the flavours of seduction and the heady aromas of change, the writers here celebrate women, food and friendship across an international kitchen table. Through a swapping of personal stories, recipes and reasons, they explore the cultural, political and deeply personal resonances that food carries for women.

Good recipes like good books are often those that come to us from someone else, recommended both for what they are and the relevance they hold in our lives. We would like to thank our contributors for sharing their own recommendations here, and fulfilling all our expectations about the creativity and community that food can bring. *Something to Savour* is a treat indeed.

Laurie Critchley and Helen Windrath
London, 1996

Clouds MICHÈLE ROBERTS

This is a delicious snack to serve with a glass of dry white wine before lunch, or as a first course. My French grandmother used to make it, as a way of using up left-over egg whites. It's one of the best things she ever cooked for us. I like associating this sensual, fluffy, frivolous dish with her, since she was a shy and reserved person. Recently, I discovered she always kept a pistol in the wardrobe. If I were a burglar, I'd break in for these.

You will need per person:

1 egg white
....
¼ cup/25g/1oz grated Gruyère cheese
....
extra virgin olive oil for frying
....
salt
....

Whip the egg whites to soft peaks. Gently fold in the grated Gruyère. Heat extra-virgin olive oil in a frying pan. Spoon in the clouds. Turn over after a minute when they are golden-brown, and fry on the other side. Serve straight away, sprinkled with salt.

NB. You *must* use extra virgin olive oil and Gruyère cheese or it doesn't taste good!

Michèle Roberts is the author of numerous bestselling novels including *A Piece of the Night* (The Women's Press, 1978) and *The Visitation* (The Women's Press, 1983). Her novel, *Daughters of the House*, was shortlisted for the Booker Prize in 1992 and won the 1993 W H Smith Literary Award. Her eighth novel, *Impossible Saints*, is published in spring 1997.

Garlic Cheese Grits LISA ALTHER

Although I grew up in the Appalachian Mountains of Tennessee, I've lived most of my adult life in New York, New England and Europe. Every time I get homesick, I make myself some grits. The first time I tried this remedy, I searched a grocery store in New York City for grits. Unable to find any, I consulted an employee who was stocking the shelves. He asked, 'Did you try the cereal section?' I nodded. 'How about the rice section?' I nodded again. 'Did you look in the foreign foods section?' In that moment I understood that my homesickness wasn't just idle nostalgia: in New Yorkers' eyes as well as my own, I was a foreigner far from home.

Eating grits reminds me of my maternal grandfather, whose family were millers in Alsace and, later, in upstate New York. It also reminds me of my paternal grand-parents, who grew up on small farms in the coal-mining region of southwest Virginia. Both had Cherokee ancestry, and grits are so essential to the Cherokees that their equiv-alent of the Eden myth centers around them: Selu, the Corn Mother, would cook grits every evening for her grandsons to eat with the turkey they had hunted. Each day she disappeared into a shed and emerged carrying a pan overflowing with grits. One day her grandsons spied on her through a crack and saw her running her hands down her sides, grits falling off her body into the pan. Disgusted, the grandsons refused to eat the grits at supper that night. Realizing her grandsons had discovered her secret, Selu announced that she would have to die. She explained to her grandsons how to plant her body in the ground and tend it so that corn would sprout from her corpse. What she had freely given them, they would now have to work for, because of the disrespect they had shown her.

The goodness of grits is about the only thing Southerners agree on. All races, classes, religions, and both genders of every sexual persuasion eat them for breakfast, lunch or dinner. Grits provide the courage to get through the working day, and the solace to go to sleep at night. Grits are to Southerners what Prozac is to other Americans.

serves 6

1 cup/150g/5oz grits (coarse oatmeal)

1 stick/115g/4oz butter

¾ cup/85g/3oz Cheddar cheese, grated

3 eggs, beaten

½ cup/125ml/4fl oz milk

½ tsp minced garlic

salt and pepper

½ cup/40g/1½ oz buttered corn flakes or bread crumbs (optional)

Cook the grits according to the directions on the box. Cool for 15 minutes. Preheat the oven to 180°C/350°F/Gas 4. Melt the butter and cheese and add to the grits. Beat the eggs with the milk and slowly stir into the grits. Add the garlic, and salt and pepper to taste. Pour into a buttered 2–quart/1.8–liter/3–pint baking dish and top, if desired, with some extra grated cheese and the corn flakes or bread crumbs. Bake for 40 minutes, or until set.

Lisa Alther was born in 1944 in Kingsport, Tennessee.

After graduating from Wellesley College in 1966, she worked for Athenum Publishers in New York before moving to Hinesburg, Vermont, where she lived for many years, raising her daughter. Having lived in London and Paris, she currently divides her time between Vermont and New York City. Described by the *New York Times Book Review* as possessing a 'comic genius', Lisa Alther is the bestselling author of five novels, *Kinflicks*, *Original Sins*, *Other Women*, *Bedrock* and *Five Minutes in Heaven*, and the novella, *Birdman and the Dancer*.

Ella Anderson's Fruit Dressing
ELLEN HART

I learned my love of food from my grandmother. The memories of her home are so rich and vivid in my mind that, even now, I can summon them at a moment's notice. My grandmother loved music, and she loved to entertain. There was always something wonderful to eat at Grandma Ella's.

On the weekends when I'd come to visit, I usually found the radio tuned to the Metropolitan opera. I enjoyed playing the grand piano in the living room, but most of all I loved to watch my grandmother cook. When I was very small, I remember helping her make Christmas Spritz cookies – one of my favorites. I can still see her trained hands, giving the cookie press just the right amount of pressure. As I grew older, I realized she never used recipes – even for her baked goods. She'd cooked for so many years with such intelligence and joy that everything was now produced by instinct. It was that instinctual sense of food that I grew to appreciate only years later, during my time as a professional chef.

And what foods she created. Norwegian meatballs. Roast turkey with all the trimmings. Thick egg noodles and chicken in a rich gravy – something she called her Chicken Hot Dish. Cinnamon buns. Lemon Schuam tortes. Floating Islands. Homemade apple pies, lemon pies, pumpkin pies. And her melt-in-the-mouth ginger bars and raisin cookies.

Although the simple yet delicious fruit dressing recipe I've chosen to share with all of you was adapted from a famous inn on the Wisconsin border, I first tried it as

8

a young child at my grandmother's house. Even today, it tastes like Thanksgiving to me. And Christmas dinner. And cousin Ray's birthday. And all the good times I spent at my grandmother's abundant table. Perhaps more to the point, the dressing reminds me of the love and warmth of a very special woman – someone I'll never forget.

makes 1pt/475ml/16fl oz

$^1/_2$ cup/100g/$3^1/_2$oz white, granulated sugar	
$^1/_4$ cup/60ml/2fl oz apple cider vinegar	
1 tbsp Worcestershire sauce	
2 tbsp grated yellow onion	
1 cup/250ml/8fl oz salad oil	
1 tsp salt	
1 tsp dry mustard	
1 tsp paprika	
2 tsp celery seed	

Whip all the ingredients together until thoroughly mixed and slightly thickened. Keep refrigerated and shake well before using.

Use as a dressing for fresh fruit – strawberries, citrus fruit, melon, blueberries, kiwi, apples, pears, plums, peaches. Cut the fruit into thin slices and place on a bed of head lettuce. Top with dressing and chill.

Ellen Hart is the author of six mysteries featuring Jane Lawless, restaurateur and sleuth, including *Stage Fright* (The Women's Press, 1994) and *A Small Sacrifice* (The Women's Press, 1995). She was a professional chef for fifteen years before becoming a full-time writer. Ellen Hart lives in Minneapolis with her partner of seventeen years, and recently became a grandmother.

Cauliflower with Five Spices and Loochies BULBUL SHARMA

Fenugreek, mustard, caraway, cumin and aniseed are thrown into the hot mustard oil. A pungent aroma wrapped in smoke rises slowly, circles Dida's head and then travels towards us. My brother and I lean forward, taking care not to fall over the invisible line that divides my grandmother's kitchen from the rest of the house. No one is allowed into this tiny, dark room which is swabbed and cleaned four times a day by Dida. Onions, garlic, meat, glass dishes and servants have never entered the room though a small brown mouse lives here and we see it sometimes peering at us behind a line of copper vessels. Dida sits and cooks on the floor of the kitchen and I see her chopping vegetables into tiny pieces, cleaning rice, kneading dough or washing spinach leaves all through the day, though she eats only once a day and fasts every other day like all orthodox Brahmin widows. Sometimes my mother is allowed into the kitchen but only after she has bathed, washed her hair and changed into fresh clothes.

Dida, who has always been frail and dressed in a widow's white saree ever since I can remember, cooks and eats before the other members of the family. The rest of us – the grandchildren, sons, daughters-in-laws and various poor relatives whom Dida likes to feed – sit around the long, marble table – which Dida never touches, though she brought it to the house as a child bride 60 years ago as a part of her dowry. The table reeks of all the things she hates. Rich red-meat curries lashed with onions and garlic have stained it; her sons have entertained around it all kinds of strange people, who were certainly not Brahmins; and once she saw a foul-smelling bottle of beer standing on it. But Dida likes to circle the polluted table, while we eat, dropping delicacies like fried eggplants (aubergines), 'loochies' and the sweets she has made before us. She always stands a little away, taking care not to touch the table. Her pale hands, which I've seen her wash at least fifty times a day, hover like dragonflies. And then, suddenly, something delicious falls on to my plate.

This cauliflower recipe, with a minimum amount of spices, pale gold and subtly flavoured, was one of Dida's favourite dishes. She would heap large amounts of cauliflower and 'loochi' for each of us on a brass plate and then slide it towards us where we sat near the kitchen door. 'Eat, eat . . . so thin you are', she would say as she watched us catch the plates like trained seals. Her simple food, without any garnish or colour, was always special because it was her way of caressing us without getting her hands polluted.

CAULIFLOWER WITH FIVE SPICES

1 tbsp cooking oil

....

$\frac{1}{2}$ tsp five-spice mixture (aniseed, caraway, cumin, mustard and fenugreek seeds mixed in equal quantities)

....

2 medium potatoes, cut into small cubes

....

1 small cauliflower, cut into sprigs

....

salt

....

Heat the oil in a wok or deep pan. Add the five-spice mixture and let it hiss and crackle. Throw in the potatoes and sauté lightly. Add the cauliflower pieces and salt to taste. Stir to mix the spices. Cover the wok or pan and cook over a low heat for 5 minutes. Take off the cover and stir frequently to make sure the vegetables are evenly cooked. The potatoes and the cauliflower pieces should be tender yet firm. Serve hot with rice or 'loochies'.

LOOCHIES

1 cup/115g/4oz/white flour
salt
1 tbsp ghee (clarified butter)
oil for deep-frying

Sift the flour and salt together. Add the ghee and knead the flour into a stiff dough, adding sufficient water. Divide the dough into seven or eight small balls and roll each one out into a thin circle. Deep fry them, one by one, in hot oil over a low heat. Take them out of the pan with a large spoon while they are crisp and white. They should be eaten at once.

Bulbul Sharma was born in 1952 and was educated at Jawaharlal Nehru University, New Delhi, following which she studied Russian literature in Moscow. She is a painter and printmaker and has held several solo exhibitions of her work over the last ten years. She is the author of two collections of short stories, *My Sainted Aunts* and *The Perfect Woman*, and her work has been anthologised in *In Other Words: New Writing by Indian Women* (The Women's Press, 1993). She currently works as an art teacher with children with disabilities, and holds monoprinting/story-telling workshops for women and children.

Nam Prik Pow (Prawn Sambal)
BETH YAHP

My Siamese grandmother was a small, dark, fierce woman who wore a uniform of batik sarungs and cotton tops she sewed herself, her hair neatly pinned into a bun. Thick golden hoops lengthened her ears. Wherever she went there was a cool smell of jasmine water, even in the kitchen, challenging the pervasive spices and oils. Mamanan came to visit when I was six, when our family moved back to Kuala Lumpur. I recall the new house filled with packing crates and the debris of moving, hired lorry men stepping in and out amongst the piled boxes and furniture so good to scramble over and hide-and-seek between. My sisters and I shrieked with laughter, sent pieces of cardboard sailing into the air, gigantic confetti. My mother, baby on one hip, a rumple of cleaning cloths on the other, was at her wit's end. Mamanan shooed us into her domain, the kitchen.

Of course she made *Nam Prik Pow* on many other occasions, as did my mother, and even I did, overseas, in mid-winter, in homesick disconsolation. But this memory persists: of Mamanan amidst the chaos of an ill-prepared kitchen, hair escaping from her bun, children swarming around her searching for wok and chopping block as directed, digging everywhere for garlic, shallots and dried prawns. My mother hovered in the doorway, baby squalling in the crook of her elbow, as we children squatted just away from the swishing chopper, the sizzling splashes of oil, watching Mamanan slice and fry and dip her face into the fragrant stream of smoke rising from the wok. The ladle she wielded with graceful dexterity, drizzling a

13

pinch of salt, a handful of pounded salt fish into the swirling mass as casually as she drizzled stories to go with her sambal on to our upturned heads. My sisters and I hugged ourselves in anticipation, awed by the magic of chillies and tamarind paste made mouth-watering, magically transformed ourselves into good, quiet, little girls. We lined buttered squares of bread on the counter, ready and waiting. The smells were dizzying, a delicious scraping to the backs of our throats. The contents of the wok hissed and spat like something alive.

500g/18oz garlic	
500g/18oz shallots (small purple Indian/sweet onions)	
15 dried chillies	
2 cups/250g/9oz dried prawns (shrimp)	
6 cups/1.4l/2½pt vegetable cooking oil	
7.5cm/3in piece of good salt fish	
6 tbsp sugar or to taste	
1 tbsp salt or to taste	
250g/9oz block tamarind paste (made into 4 cups/1l/1¾ pt of very thick tamarind water)	

Peel and wash the garlic and shallots. Cut into thin slices and put separately on a big tray. Wash the chillies and dried prawns but don't mix them. Dry in the sun or in a slow oven.

Heat the oil in a wok. First fry the garlic until brown and crisp. Drain on to greased paper. Do the same with the shallots and chillies. Fry the salt fish last.

Pound the fried dried prawns, chillies, garlic, shallots and salt fish until fine. Put the pounded ingredients back in the heated wok. Add the sugar, salt and tamarind water. Fry over a slow heat until dry. Then leave to cool and put into a jar. It is ready to eat.

14

The Thais use Nam Prik Pow in most of their cuisine, including prawn soup (*tom yam*) and seafood salad. Spread on bread, it makes a very delicious sandwich.

Beth Yahp was born in Malaysia in 1964 and moved to Australia in 1984. Her short fiction, essays and articles have been widely published and her novel, *The Crocodile Fury* (The Women's Press, 1996), won the Victorian Premier's Prize for First Fiction and the Ethnic Affairs Commission Award. It has since been translated and published in Singapore, the Netherlands, Belgium and Spain.

Hope You Luck — Chinese Mochi Donuts (Jin Dui) KATHLEEN TYAU

Jin dui is a deep-fried dumpling served as a Chinese New Year's treat. When I was a child, I watched my popo (grandmother) make *jin dui*, watched her press the dumplings into hot peanut oil with the back of a slotted wire spoon with a long bamboo handle. The dumplings sizzled and popped and miraculously puffed until they were large, round balls, brown and crisp on the outside. When we bit into the dumpling, our mouths filled with sweet, chewy rice dough and the savory taste of barbecued pork or the sweet flavor of coconut, plus the pervasive flavor of peanuts throughout. Since I helped Popo, I got to eat the *jin dui* fresh out of the kettle, still warm and round, with its shockingly delicate crispness. Cold *jin dui* lost its puffiness and crisp texture.

My mother gave me this recipe years ago. She got the recipe from my popo, who used rice bowls, tea cups, and whiskey jiggers to measure ingredients (if she bothered to measure at all). My cousin Gary reminded me of this recipe when I visited him in Washington state recently. He said, 'Your mother made the best *jin dui*.' He wants the recipe, so he can make some. I want to make *jin dui* too. I even went out and bought a box of mochi flour.

If only I had the slotted wire spoon. I saw this spoon in my mother's kitchen cupboard recently. I felt the dark bamboo handle, still oily, and the flavors and texture of *jin dui* came back to me. Unfortunately, I failed to save the spoon from being hauled off to a thrift shop after my parents died. Perhaps if I had this spoon, I would have the right touch. Both my mother and Popo insisted that the art

16

of *jin dui* lay in the pressing of the dumplings into the hot oil with the appropriate touch and for the right number of times. My mother knew this would not be easy. Thus her words: '*Hope you luck.*' She underscored the words because she knew that the cooking of *jin dui* required more than a recipe. I think of my popo, how she brought this recipe with her from China, probably from her own mother, whom she never saw again after moving to Hawaii. My popo was a generous woman and an excellent cook, like my own mother, and I know they would not mind my sharing this recipe. But the right touch, the luck? How do I convey these essential ingredients? How will I find them myself?

JIN DUI (CHINESE MOCHI DONUTS)

3 rice bowls of *mochi* flour

1 rice bowl of coarse brown sugar

1–1½ rice bowls of water or less

1 soup spoon whiskey

1 tsp vinegar

sesame seeds

oil for frying

Mix the *mochi* flour and brown sugar together with your hands and add 1 rice bowl of water with the whiskey and vinegar to the dry ingredients. Mix the dough, adding about ½ rice bowl more water, until the dough is like pie crust mixture. *Do not knead.* Then form into balls and stuff with the meat or coconut filling. Roll in sesame seeds and deep-fry in medium hot oil (180–200°C/375–400°F). Press the balls after 30 seconds – the more you press, the bigger they get. *Hope you luck* – continue pressing for about 8 to 10 minutes.

MEAT FILLING

½ cup/75g/2½oz ham or *char siu* (red barbecued pork), diced small

½ cup/50g/2oz roast peanuts

1 tbsp green onions

1 tsp Chinese parsley (cilantro)

COCONUT FILLING

½ cup/40g/1½oz grated coconut

½ cup/50g/2oz crushed roast peanuts

3 tbsp sugar

Kathleen Tyau is Chinese-Hawaiian and grew up on the island of Oahu. She is the author of numerous short stories and the novel, *A Little Too Much is Enough* (The Women's Press, 1996). She currently lives in Oregon.

Kreplach ELLEN GALFORD

Chinese grandmothers make *won-tons*; Siberian grandmothers make *pelmeny*; Italian grandmothers make *ravioli*; Jewish grandmothers make *kreplach*. These little savoury dumplings travelled the ancient trade routes of Eurasia, carried along with the amber, the spices, the silks, the folktales, the migrating tribes. Give or take some variations in the filling, there's little difference between them: little envelopes of soft dough wrapped round a stuffing.

For the Jewish New Year, my maternal grandmother, Annie Broadman, turned out *kreplach* by the hundreds for our very large, hungry and sociable clan of aunts, uncles, and cousins several times removed. Some *kreplach* would be simmered in the chicken soup; others (renamed *varennikes*, and stuffed with potato instead of meat) would be boiled and slathered with sour cream and butter; the rest would be baked in a glaze of honey as *saltenusses*, a dish whose strange savoury–sweetness must go back a thousand years or more.

When I was little, I'd watch her make *kreplach* in our kitchen in New Jersey. The recipe, if any, was in her head; weights and measures were quite irrelevant. 'How do you know how much to put in?' I'd ask. 'You just put in enough,' she'd answer. An initiation into the mysteries.

Her instructions to me, I'm quite sure, were the same, word for word, that Annie's mother Sarah had given her, sometime circa 1900, in their crowded flat in the Hell's Kitchen district of Manhattan, and Sarah's mother (whose name I don't know, but who married the son of a woman called – like my own mother – Leah) had given Sarah in a little wooden house in the old Baltic province of Kovno Gubernia, sometime in the 1870s.

To start your *kreplach* dough, said each of these mothers in their turn, put the flour ('Enough') on to a board and 'make a well'. The first time I heard that, and every time I've done it for myself, one particular well has floated into my mind's eye: the biblical one where Abraham's servant, in search of a bride for Isaac, met Rebekah. Now I'm sure this Rebekah was a woman of many virtues, but I'll bet her *kreplach* weren't half as good as Annie's.

KREPLACH DOUGH

makes about 2 dozen (quantities, needless to say, are all 'more or less')

2¾ cups/300g/11oz/plain (all-purpose) white flour (unsifted)
2 eggs, lightly beaten
1 tbsp water
½ tsp salt

Place the flour on a board and make a well in the middle of it. Pour in the eggs, water and salt, and work them quickly into the flour (using one hand only if you want to do it Annie's way) until it forms a dough. Knead until smooth and elastic, then roll out into a sheet, thin enough to fold and shape easily but not so paper-thin that it becomes too fragile for filling. Cut the sheet into squares (about 7.5cm/3in), and place 1 tablespoonful (more or less) of filling on to the centre of each. Fold each square into a triangle, enclosing the filling, moistening your fingers with a bit of water and pinching the edges to seal them shut.

Drop the kreplach into a large potful of boiling soup (traditionally a clear chicken broth, though a vegetable broth would be fine too) or well salted boiling water and cook – at a moderate, not-too-violent boil – until they float to the surface – about 20 minutes. Either serve in chicken (or clear vegetable) soup, or drain very well and fry in oil or butter.

KREPLACH FILLINGS

For the carnivorous:

Sauté 1 finely chopped onion in a little vegetable oil until golden brown. Mix it thoroughly with 2 cups/250g/8oz finely minced cooked chicken or beef, 1 egg yolk, $1/2$–$3/4$ tsp salt, a few grindings of black pepper, and 1 tbsp finely chopped parsley.

For vegetarians:

This is a 'dairy' filling, traditionally served with sour cream and – (but only for the truly sybaritic – lashings of melted butter.) Sauté 1 finely chopped onion in 3 tbsp/40g/ $1^1/2$ oz/butter. Mix it with $1^3/4$cups/350g/12oz mashed potatoes, 1 cup/125g/$4^1/2$oz very well-drained small curd cottage cheese, 1 egg, 1 tsp salt and a few grindings of black pepper.

Ellen Galford was born in New Jersey, USA, but has lived for most of the past quarter century in Scotland. If ethnic definitions are needed, she defines herself as an Ashkenazic Jewish heretic and adopted Scot. Her novels include *Moll Cutpurse: Her True History*, *Queendom Come*, *The Dyke and the Dybbuk* (winner of a Lambda Literary Award) and *The Fires of Bride* (The Women's Press, 1986).

Krautsvekel by E-Mail
SUZY McKEE CHARNAS

E-mail, Suzy Charnas in New Mexico to Shuli B. in Jerusalem (we had met through a discussion of a novella of mine on a mailing list of psychiatrists and psychologists who are interested in psychology in the arts):

Dear Shuli,

Do you cook a dish called (sorry, don't know if the spelling is correct) '*krautsvekel*'? I am thinking of sending a recipe for it to my British publisher for inclusion in a book of recipes from their authors, but I haven't got it written down anywhere and have not made *krautsvekel* for years.

My New Yorker mother learned to make it from her Viennese, Jewish mother, and all questions to either of them about quantities or other minor details of cooking were met with the traditional responses, i.e.: 'You have to use *enough*', or, 'a good shake', or 'just add a *schlook* of red wine'. Not that my mother made this dish very often, or any dish; she was a working woman, a freelance artist in textile design with two daughters to raise on her own, and we generally ate stew or lamb chops that we cooked ourselves.

In fact, my grandmother had also raised her kids on her own, having kicked her husband out for hanging around doing nothing while she worked in the twine shop of her uncle in Minneapolis (my grandfather was not exactly doing nothing; he was studying Torah, like a good Jewish head–of–household, while his wife took care of worldly things like the house and the kids). Her

22

mother had also somehow or other given her nominal man the boot, so perhaps it was not surprising that in her turn my mother asked my father to leave because he was the most passive (living) human being on the face of the earth and she was full of vim and ambition; the strain of providing all the energy in the marriage was killing her.

So all these guys had to go get their *krautsvekel* elsewhere.

I seem to recall that this dish was made by mixing noodles, sautéed cabbage (we said 'fried' in those days), and cottage cheese. What I can't remember is whether or not the dish included any onions or garlic. Can you help me out here?

Dear Suzy,
I use onions and lots of ground pepper when I make this. At what stage do you add the cottage cheese?

Dear Shuli,
That's the kind of thing that *you're* supposed to be telling me.

Dear Suzy,
I always serve the cottage cheese separately, on the side. How come you have not been feeding *krautsvekel* to your family all this time?

Dear Shuli,
It's worse than that. I had actual written recipes (taken down reporter-style, on the spot from observation) for lots of great things my grandmother used to cook: *knockerel* (yummy little soft dumplings named after your knuckle bones), *schlischkel* (soft, cylindrical potato noodles fried in butter-soaked breadcrumbs), and of course blintzes, served stuffed with slightly sweetened

cottage cheese and topped with a little sour cream and a cinnamon and sugar dusting. I threw those recipes away.

It was all wonderful, and it all inevitably included things like half a cup of sugar, a stick of butter, or a pint of sour cream. The results are lethal (or so the current wisdom has it; my grandmother lived to be 84); they are so good that you can't eat just a modest portion; and there is no way in the world to make a 'lowfat' version of a butter-soaked, breadcrumb-encrusted potato noodle.

So here in the land of skinny work-out mavens this recipe for *krautsvekel* falls into the category of a museum piece:

Boil up a bowl of broad, flat egg noodles (pasta didn't have names in those days unless you were Italian), rinse them so they don't stick, and set them aside. Cook them *al dente* so they won't turn to mush in the cooking they will receive further along.

In a big, deep skillet, fry a batch of fresh, sweet cabbage, chopped (with onions if you wish), in butter until the vegetables start to brown. Good cabbage is selected by weight; the heavier the head for its size, the sweeter and juicier it will be.

Dump in the noodles, add butter, and stir the whole thing around over a medium flame till it's hot. Spoon in plenty of cottage cheese and stir some more; the cheese will cook into lumps and crumbles. This is a rather messy-looking dish, but tasty. Add salt to taste, and serve.

Come to think of it, all the aforementioned ladies – great grandmother, grandmother, and mom – were built on the short, stoutish middle-European model, their rather fire-pluggish forms well stuffed no doubt with cream, eggs, sugar, and butter. It was probably using the strength given them by such hearty food as *schlischkel* and *krautsvekel* that they took their lives and their kids' lives into their own hands and made their way in the world *sans* husbands, in eras when women were not quick to do that. Maybe if I ate such food now, my own far from svelte figure would be less wobbly and a lot stronger. On the other hand, my marriage is going strong after 27 years.

Shuli, what is a *schlook*?

Dear Suzy,
A *schlook* is a dollop of anything wet enough to be poured; it's a lot like *enough*.

Suzy McKee Charnas was born in 1939. Her bestselling novels include *The Vampire Tapestry* (1992), winner of the Nebula Award, 1980, *The Furies* (1995), *Walk to the End of the World* and *Motherlines* (1989) — all published by The Women's Press. She has had one stage play produced, is looking for a production for a new play — about being married to the phantom of the opera — and has recently revised the lyrics for a stage musical based on the film, *Nosferatu*. Suzy McKee Charnas also writes short stories and novels for young adults. She lives in New Mexico.

Pork or Chick-peas with Red Peppers LESLIE WILSON

When I was small, I used to dream of living in Austria, as my mother did in her childhood. She did magical things, she rode, she had her voice trained, she got to know the singers at the Graz Opera. And she had wonderful food to eat. Omi, my grandmother, cooked it. Polenta, fresh noodles, goulasch, and especially pork with lots of sweet peppers. Omi came to live with us when I was a child, and she could chop vegetables better than anyone else in the world, but she'd become a sad religious recluse, a vegetarian, and never cooked. Though she still made wonderful dark sourdough bread.

Last time I was in Vienna, I bought a kilogram of pointy peppers from a street market on the day I left. I carried them back to Reading, Berkshire, and sat down with my beautiful and food-loving friend Tamara, who is half Italian and half Russian, to see if we could reinvent one of my grandmother's recipes. We laughed a lot, drank Italian white wine, spent a long time slivering peppers, and made polenta to go with the dish, which celebrates my nostalgia for the Austrian child I might have been and for my grandmother's years of liveliness and pleasure, which I never saw. The great thing about this recipe is that if your household, like mine, contains a vegetarian, you can set aside a portion for them before the meat goes in. If you're cash-strapped, you can do the peasant-thing: use a small portion of pork for flavour, and a lot of chick-peas for protein.

serves 4

4 or more large red (bell) peppers and 1 green (bell) pepper, quartered lengthwise, deseeded and destalked, then fine-sliced crosswise

1 hot pepper, chopped as fine as you can (or a pinch of chilli powder just to add bite)

can chopped tomatoes, or 500g/18oz fresh tomatoes, skinned and chopped

1 large onion, 1 stick celery, centre portion of 1 thin leek, all fine-chopped

4 cloves garlic, crushed

½ tsp sugar

1 tsp cumin

1 tsp coriander

1 tsp powdered paprika

fresh lovate or fresh flat-leaf parsley, coarse-chopped

dried or fresh basil

dried thyme

vegetable oil (extra virgin olive helps) for frying

stock (bouillon) cube or 1 tsp thick jellied chicken stock

425g/15oz can chick-peas (garbanzo beans)

500g/18oz lean pork

First, set your oven moderately high (190°C/375°F/Gas 5 or 170°C for fan-assisted ovens). Also, prepare all the vegetables before you start and put them together in a bowl. In as large and heavy a pan as you have, dry-roast the cumin and coriander, then tip them out and grind them to a powder. (If you forget to do this, give them 2 minutes on full power in a microwave.) Put the paprika and dry herbs in the pan with them (and the pinch of chilli if you're using powder). In the same pan, fry the garlic, onion, leeks, celery, peppers, chillis (if you're using them) and fresh herbs in the oil for about 5 minutes, stirring from time to time. Don't add the tomatoes until the peppers *et al* are really soft. Add the stock cube or jellied stock, dried herbs and spices, and the chick-peas. Keep frying until the liquid has decreased by about a quarter.

Butter an ovenproof dish and put the pepper mixture into it. Vegetarians need do no more than bake this concoction for 10 minutes and then serve (with either polenta, rice or noodles and sour cream, natural yoghurt or Parmesan cheese). Carnivores, however, must set to slicing again. Cut the pork as thin as you can stand after all that pepper-chopping, then fry it right through, really fast. Sling it in with the pepper mixture, give it a good stir so that the pork is red with sauce and bake for 10 minutes. Serve with polenta or rice or . . . (but you've already heard this *vis-à-vis* my veggie version) – enjoy!

If you're skint for wine, I recommend Grüner Veltliner (an Austrian vintage, but the one I get from my local supermarket is made in Hungary). If you want to splash out and can get hold of it, Lacrima Christi de Vesuvio tastes like bottled sunshine. I'd also recommend any good Alsatian wine or else a nice velvety Italian red.

Leslie Wilson's mother was German but lived for most of her childhood in Graz, Austria. Her father was English. She is the author of *Mourning Is Not Permitted* (The Women's Press, 1990), *Malefice*, (Picador, 1992 and 1994) and *The Mountain of Immoderate Desires* (Weidenfeld and Nicolson, 1994, and Phoenix, 1995).

Couscous MARIE CARDINAL

At home in the country in Algeria the kitchen was a room with windows which overlooked the kitchen garden on one side and the yard on the other. Here, once a week, the women used to celebrate the great couscous ritual. This was in the very distant past, in my childhood.

There was Zoubida, Bahia, Aicha, Kader's two girls, and me.

Kheira, the high priestess of couscous, slipped cushions under the little girls' behinds so that they could sit with a good view of the proceedings. The huge pale oak table stretched before them, empty for the moment.

We all had knives in our hands; we were ready.

Then Youssef, the gardener, placed in the centre of the table a basket filled with courgettes (zucchini), aubergines (eggplants), onions, carrots, swede (rutabaga), peppers and tomatoes, all freshly picked from the garden. Underneath these were an enormous, leafy head of celery, a bunch of coriander (cilantro), some thyme and some bay leaves. The basket's aroma promised certain delight.

Meanwhile old Kheira had put the chick-peas (garbanzo beans) and the raisins to soak – muscady grape raisins that she had kept from the last harvest. Her mother, Daïba, spent whole summers drying fruit – her speciality. Figs, grapes and little green and red pimentos would be laid out on a fine grate. She would keep watch over them with fastidious care: they were not to be crowded together or touching, the air had to circulate above and below; they were to be neither in direct sunlight, nor too much in the shade. She hustled the children if they went near, and would move the fruit and pimentos around often, following the path of the sun. Once dried, her figs and grapes were moist, sugary and delicious, and her pimentos took the roof off your mouth.

Old Kheira, dressed in her finest *haïk*, travelled into town in grandmother's car, driven by Kader. She spent a long time at the butcher's choosing plates of cutlets and four necklaces of lamb which she had cut into thick slices so that the meat wouldn't disintegrate as it cooked. Before she had set off she had asked Aoued to kill a couple of plump chickens – two pretentious roosters.

It would be a lamb and chicken couscous for everyone on the farm: some twenty people.

To work!

First of all the onions were peeled and cut into big rounds. Kheira turned them a golden colour in a little olive oil and then added the meat to brown, on a low heat. Meanwhile the girls prepared the vegetables: 'the least juicy first, tomatoes last'. Aubergines were first of all, peeled and cut into big cubes, then carrots, turnips, celery and courgettes, all duly prepared. Where vegetables were small and tender, they were left whole, except for the peppers which were cut open, their seeds removed, and sliced into biggish strips. Then the tomatoes, halved or quartered. Everything was tipped little by little into the cooking pots where, up until now, the meat had been simmering. Lastly, Kheira added thyme, coriander, bay leaf and covered everything in water. 'It smells good, children,' she declared.

In the final stages the chick-peas also went into the stock. 'Above all don't forget the chick-peas.'

She had already laid the table with a large white linen table-cloth on to which she scattered the dry couscous semolina. She busied herself, bustling to and from the stove to the table. Dipping her hands into a bowl of salted water she sprinkled the dry couscous in an energetic

30

repetitive movement. 'This is to make it swell up,' she announced for the girls' sake. Afterwards, she took large handfuls and put them into the couscous colander that she perched over the steam rising from the pots where the meat and vegetable stock was gently cooking. She then covered the couscous and, with the help of some damp cloths, stopped up all the colander holes: 'The steam must only rise upwards.'

The girls cleaned the table, set the dishes and serving pots, and two separate bowls into which they put the soaked raisins, and the finely ground pimentos. At the very last moment they covered each one with stock to make a hot and a mild sauce.

Kheira had meanwhile brought out a deep wooden dish. When she deemed the couscous had swelled up enough she poured it into this dish. It was burning hot and steaming, yellow and white.

Kheira then plunged her hands, with their reddened palms, into the hot couscous. With magnificent dexterity she began rolling it between her fingers to remove even the slightest trace of lumpiness. Soon every grain was separated. Next she put it back into the colander to make it swell up a little more. She rolled it in her fingers again, this time adding a very tiny amount of butter. When she put it back on to the steam, for a last and final cook, the couscous glistened.

A whole morning had passed.

At that point someone rang the bell. We soon heard sounds from the yard: the men putting the horses and carts away. 'I'm starving!' Uncle shouted as he climbed the stairs four by four.

Note: You can buy couscous semolina pre-cooked. All you have to do is steam it over some boiling stock to make it swell up and try to avoid it clumping together.

Marie Cardinal was born in Algeria in 1929. She is the author of the classic and internationally bestselling novel of psychoanalysis, *The Words to Say It* (The Women's Press, 1993) which won the Prix Littré and has been translated into over twelve languages worldwide. Other novels include *Devotion and Disorder* (The Women's Press, 1991). Her non-fiction works include her recent collection of writings on feminism, philosophy, literature and psycho-analysis, *In Other Words* (The Women's Press, 1996).

Translated from the French by Joanna Rabiger

Koussa Mishi (Stuffed Courgettes) HANAN AL-SHAYKH

They are Mediterranean courgettes: pale green, lime lemonade, hazel green, exactly the colour of the novelist Donna Tartt's eyes.

I have always been attracted to this vegetable which where I come from has always been associated with a certain magical atmosphere, as well as several suggestive stories. This is true even of its name which becomes 'cunt' in Arabic if the letter 'o' is removed as we used to do when children.

Whenever courgettes were being prepared for a meal, all the women of the household would scatter the cut top of this vegetable (called *fezes*) on their foreheads. For some strange reason, these *fezes* would hold on to the skin like a magnet, and pull and smooth the forehead lines and wrinkles. To my childhood eyes, the *fezes* made the women look like extra-terrestrial beings wearing air conditioning units for their faces while cooking in hot kitchens. Then there were the devoted, religiously pious women who would exclaim while scooping out the pulp of the courgettes: 'God forgive me! I am innocent of what my act might suggest! I am just preparing stuffed courgettes!'

But the main story about stuffed courgettes is that of the sexually deprived wife who asked a white witch to prescribe her husband a potion in order to satisfy her. But the anxious wife sprinkled the potion on the food she was preparing instead of sprinkling it on her husband's dish. That is why she was mortified when she lifted the lid and saw the stuffed courgettes entering the stuffed vine leaves exactly like a man enters a woman.

serves 4

10 large Mediterranean courgettes (zucchini)
1 cup/225g/8oz lean ground lamb
1 cup/50g/2oz rice, washed and drained
2 tsp olive oil
$\frac{1}{2}$ tsp ground cinnamon
$1\frac{1}{4}$ tsp allspice
salt and pepper
3 chopped ripe tomatoes
$1\frac{1}{4}$ cups/300ml/$\frac{1}{2}$pt water
$1\frac{1}{4}$ cups/300ml/$\frac{1}{2}$pt tomato juice

Cut off the tops of the courgettes (the *fezes*). Gently scoop out the pulp of each courgette with a special courgette scooper – or a teaspoon will do.

In a separate bowl, mix the lamb with the rice and add the olive oil, cinnamon, allspice, and some salt and pepper. Fill or stuff each courgette loosely with the mixture, put into a pan and sprinkle with the chopped tomato. Pour on the water and tomato juice.

Cover with a china plate, upside down so as to hold the courgettes tightly in place, and bring to the boil. Remove the plate, cover with the lid, and then simmer for 40–50 minutes.

Hanan al-Shaykh is considered by many to be one of the foremost contemporary writers in Arabic. She wrote her first novel at the age of 18 while studying in Cairo. She has since published two short story collections and five novels including *The Story of Zahra, Women of Sand and Myrrh* (selected as one of the 50 Best Books of 1992 by

Publishers Weekly and winner of the 1993 *Elle* Literary Prize) and, most recently, *Beirut Blues*. Her work has also been performed at the Hampstead Theatre in London. Since 1982, primarily because of the civil war in Lebanon, Hanan al-Shaykh has lived in London with her husband and two children.

Ash-e Reshteh (Iranian Soup)
GOHAR KORDI

'Reshteh' in Farsi is an extraordinarily rich word and is used extensively in literature and poetry. It weaves together the whole fabric of the culture. It has many, many meanings, from fibre, field, line, string, series, or tie, to versify, compose or connect. *Reshteh* also means subject of study, train or line of thought, and range of mountains. 'Ash' in Farsi means soup. For the poor people *ash* constitutes the main meal of the day, but for the rich it is only a starter.

There are many kinds of *ash* in Iran, and according to popular belief it has spiritual value and healing properties. It is usually made at gatherings as people pray around it and women often make a wish as they take turns stirring it. *Ash* is made for various purposes, such as making special vows, giving thanks for recovery from serious illness, or averting a major disaster such as famine, drought or plague. These special vows are also made on specific days, such as on the last Wednesday of the year (*chaharshanbeh soori* – the New Year's festival). They are usually made in the name of a saint, a holy person or a sacred tree or object. *Ash* is also made for travellers. 'Ash-e poshte pa' means 'for the safe return of the traveller'. Three to five days after the departure, *ash-e reshteh* is made and distributed in the neighbourhood, to avert any danger and ensure the safe return of the traveller, and family and friends are invited to come and share it. In Iran, *ash* reflects people's cultural, ethnic and religious beliefs.

serves 6

1 cup/200g/7oz kidney beans, chick-peas (garbanzo beans) and lentils, in equal amounts
5 cups/250g/9oz fresh spinach (frozen could also be used)
2 medium-sized leeks
2 cups/100g/3½oz parsley, coriander (cilantro) and dill, in equal amounts
2 cloves garlic
1 large onion
½ tbsp plain (all-purpose) flour
¼ cup/60ml/2fl oz cold water
3 tbsp cooking oil (preferably olive oil)
¼ tsp turmeric
salt and pepper
100g/3½oz egg noodles
1 tbsp chopped fresh mint (dried mint could be substituted)
6 tbsp kashk (reconstituted dried yoghurt, available from Middle Eastern groceries – natural yoghurt or vinegar to taste can be substituted)

Wash and soak the pulses (legumes). Soak them overnight (especially the beans and the chick-peas) if possible, otherwise a few hours is enough. If fresh spinach is used, it should be washed and chopped. Wash and finely chop the leeks, parsley, coriander and dill. Peel and chop the garlic and the onion. Dissolve the flour in the cold water.

Cover and boil the beans and peas gently in plenty of water until they are half cooked. Add the lentils and let them boil until they are all cooked. Fry the onion and the garlic in 2 tbsp of the oil and add the turmeric. Add three quarters of the mixture to the pulses and keep the rest aside. Add the spinach, leeks, coriander, parsley, dill and salt. Let it boil gently, uncovered, for 5 minutes. Then add the noodles and the flour paste. Reduce the heat and stir constantly for a few minutes so that the noodles do not stick. Let it boil uncovered on a low heat for a further

10 minutes, stirring occasionally. Heat the remaining oil and stir in the chopped fresh mint. Turn off the heat immediately because the mint burns easily.

Serve the soup, adding a tablespoon of kashk, yoghurt or vinegar to each serving. (If kashk is used, it should have been boiled for 20 minutes beforehand.) Dot with the remaining fried onion and garnish with the fried mint. Add salt and pepper to taste. '*Nooshe jan*', '*Bon appétit*'.

'*I shall break the strand of the love between us so that the strand may be knotted and bring me closer to you.*' (From a Farsi poem)

Gohar Kordi is the author of the autobiographical novel, *An Iranian Odyssey*, and *Mahi's Story* (The Women's Press, 1995). Her writing has appeared in numerous anthologies including *Mustn't Grumble: Writing by Disabled Women* (The Women's Press, 1994). Gohar Kordi was born and brought up in a small village in Iran and now lives in London with her husband and son.

Vegetable Soup   SLAVENKA DRAKULIĆ

My husband says that I don't know how to cook. I believe
it is true. I prepare only very simple food: soups, salads,
vegetable sautés, pasta, grilled fish and boiled or fried
meat, if I must. My recipes are the most simple ones and
I can count them – they number up to twenty perhaps at
most. Almost all of them came from my mother, even
though I left home when I was sixteen and actually had
no time to learn how to cook. I would just remember
the taste of a particular food she used to prepare, and then
try to recreate it myself. The trial and error method, I
guess. Sometimes, in the middle of my cooking, I still
phone her to ask what to do next . . .

My husband also claims that my mother is a great cook
because she belongs to a generation of women who still
know how to make *a real meal* – tasty, sophisticated, good-
looking food. Modern women no longer have the time
or interest, it's the price of emancipation – he laments.
Nowadays they mostly eat some sort of salad. Imagine, a
salad – he says. But my mother was a working woman,
too. Yet, it was unimaginable for her not to know how
to cook for at least two reasons. In a patriarchal country
such as Yugoslavia, she was expected to do all the cooking,
as well as the housework, and I do not remember seeing
my father anywhere near a kitchen stove, even once. The
second reason was communism. Living in a communist
country, you needed to know how to cook, there was no
half-prepared, canned or frozen food. On the contrary,
there was scarcity of food and you had to be more skilled,
more imaginative than an ordinary woman in the West.

Besides, people could rarely afford to eat in a restaurant. In my childhood, this would happen perhaps once a year and then it was a big family feast. So my mother was in fact forced to cook.

Luckily, a talent for good cooking runs in my mother's family, like a talent for music or painting runs in other families. She inherited it from her mother, who was well known for her kitchen. But it seems that the talent jumped over me, although I raised my daughter on my 'bad' cooking, and she survived it without visible damage. I also had to cook every day when she was born because, in 1968, there was still no baby-food available, and there was no way to feed us decently except by preparing food myself.

I too am a working woman like my mother, but I have a different attitude to food and cooking. My husband calls it disinterest but it is more complex than that, although my mother says that even as a baby I was extremely difficult to feed. My grandma had to entertain me with a box of buttons. If I noticed I was being fed, I would get angry and throw it all on the floor. However, when I was thirty years old doctors found that I had a degenerative kidney disease and immediately put me on a special low-protein, no salt diet. I was very disciplined, but to no avail. After a year or so I decided to try a macrobiotic diet, but this failed too and weak and emaciated, I ended up in hospital, in a chemo–dialysis unit three times a week. Doctors changed my diet again: I was to eat a lot of proteins (meat) but avoid fruit and vegetables. The most important change was that I had to reduce my intake of liquid, in other words, drink as little as I could. I had to physically and psychologically adapt to that.

After six long years of living on a dialysis machine that filtered my blood from accumulated poisons and learning not to be thirsty, I had a kidney transplant in 1986. After the operation doctors told me that I needed even more meat, so for the next six months I ate one pound of beefsteak per day. The big change was that I was now supposed to drink at least two litres of liquid a day. I had to retrain myself, slowly and with patience, because it was difficult to get used to drinking again. I could finally eat what I wanted, meat as well as vegetables and fruits, even bananas and chocolate that had been forbidden before because of their high calcium content. It was a great victory, a great feeling of freedom.

But not a complete freedom. Ever since my illness, instead of being associated with pleasure and joy, food in my mind is forever connected with health, with training and discipline, with *must* and *should not*, with effort, pain and radical changes in diet. I like eating, but it does not matter so much what I eat or sometimes if I even eat at all. Yet a vegetable soup is one of the things I can eat always, and enjoy, always. Soup is very important in my part of the world: it warms you up, it fills up your stomach when you have nothing else to eat, it heals you when you are sick, it keeps you company when you are lonely. It could be a beef soup with home-made noodles, a thin chicken soup for the elderly and sick, a winter potato soup, minestrone or fish soup . . . In my childhood every lunch began with a soup, often a fish or vegetable soup because no meat was available or it was too expensive. On Sundays we would get chicken soup or beef soup if it was a holiday.

This vegetable soup is of course my mother's recipe. I've eaten it throughout my childhood and my period of illness, with more or less salt; and more or less richness; making it thicker or less thick. I cooked it for my daughter while she was growing up and today, when she stays with me, she asks me to cook it for her again. When I visit my mother, she makes this soup for me too. It connects three women of three generations, always made exactly the same way, with the same ingredients. It is essential in keeping us together. And guess what? It works for men, as well. Even my husband, a hopeless gourmet, likes it, too!

A vegetable soup is incredibly simple to prepare and incredibly cheap. All you need are the same vegetables that you usually put in a beef soup, plus potatoes; an onion, two carrots, a piece of celery root, a parsley root, a bit of garlic and a leaf or two of cabbage, and a bit of leek if there is one. First chop the onion, carrot, parsley root and celery and let them sauté for about 10 minutes in a covered pot with a bit of salt and a spoonful of oil. Then add about a litre (4 cups/1³/₄pt) of water, three medium-sized potatoes cut in small cubes, a little more garlic, and finally the chopped cabbage leaves and leek, and let the soup simmer for about 35 minutes. At the end, put in a half of a teaspoon of tomato purée and let it boil for another 5 or 6 minutes. My mother has a particular trick to make this soup very tasty: at the very end, she adds a bit of Parmesan cheese cut in small pieces, but it could be any hard cheese you have at hand. If she wants the soup to be very thick – if it is the only meal – then she also beats a whole egg and pours it into the soup. Eat it warm. It will make you feel good.

Slavenka Drakulić is a Croatian writer and journalist. Her novels include *Marble Skin* (1994) and *Holograms of Fear* (1993) – both published by The Women's Press. She is also the author of the non-fiction books, *How We Survived Cmmunism and Even Laughed*, *Balkan Express* and most recently, *Café Europa*. Her latest novel is *The Taste of a Man*. Slavenka Drakulić lives between Croatia, Austria and Sweden.

Zeera Rasam GITHA HARIHARAN

What does a mother's medicine taste like? Or put another way, what is the flavour of homegrown love? Sour enough to bring back to life dead taste buds; sharp enough to melt down the hard lump of misery in the chest and the head and the nose; and pungent enough to assure you that no germ is a match for your mother's brew, her flaming peppery stream of love.

I learned this answer as a child though no one has ever asked me the question. Every time one of us children was sick and imprisoned in bed, my mother would put her special germ-chasing *rasam* on to simmer. The ingredients for her *zeera rasam* were simple and functional. There was a small sticky ball of dark tamarind; its job was to penetrate a fur-lined tongue and revive its sense of taste. Half a teaspoon of *zeera* (cumin) powder and some salt pandered to the newly awakened taste buds and assured them that life was still worth living. A pinch of turmeric purified the path of this return journey. The star, of course, was dramatic: a teaspoon of black pepper powder. To unify these individualistic flavours into a new and potent one, the secret was patience; the liquid had to be simmered until it was half its original quantity. The result was an experience to savour: a heady aroma in the kitchen, a sharp, cleansing flavour on the tongue, and a sense of reassurance that crept over you like a pair of warm, maternal arms.

Though my own children are growing up in a world that tells them that a mother's treat has to be sweet and sugary, I find myself sneaking an occasional spicy *rasam* into their special-day menu. This is how my mother's *zeera rasam* is made:

Squeeze out a small ball of tamarind that has been soaked in warm water. Add turmeric, cumin powder, freshly ground pepper and salt to the tamarind juice. Simmer till the concoction is reduced to half; then add water and bring to a boil. To season the *rasam*, add a pinch of mustard seeds, cumin seeds and a few *kadipattha* (curry) leaves that have been fried together in a teaspoon of ghee or clarified butter. Cover the mixture immediately so that the fresh aroma – like all precious, intoxicating fragrances – does not vanish.

Githa Hariharan was born in Bangalore, South India; educated in Bombay, Manila and the United States; and currently lives in New Delhi with her partner and two sons. Her début novel, *The Thousand Faces of Night* (The Women's Press, 1996), won the Commonwealth Writers Prize for the best first novel. She is also the author of a collection of short stories, *The Art of Dying*; another novel, *The Ghosts of Vasu Master*; and her work has been anthologised in *In Other Words: New Writing by Indian Women* (The Women's Press, 1993).

Potato-Cheese Soup JOAN BARFOOT

When my mother died, one of the most common remarks made about her life had to do with what a grand cook she had been. She was, in fact, so excellent in the kitchen that I never learned to be. My job was to appreciate the love contained in the raisin and lemon meringue pies, the chocolate and banana cakes, the piled plates of date-filled oatmeal cookies.

It was understood I would have to find my own, other ways to demonstrate affection and care. Food was hers. Leaving aside the variously sad and happy quests undertaken in pursuit of those other ways, one result was that when I grew up and left home, I was not at all sure exactly how water gets boiled.

Thus people who come to my dinner table find themselves facing a menu awesomely limited in range of food, but compensatingly broad, I hope, in laughter, gossip, wine, and conversation. Food, always symbolic as well as concrete, becomes a standard (or hurdle) of friendship: if people will eat at my house, it must be because they want to be with me, and if I produce food, it must be because I truly desire their company. This is an odd mutation of my mother's theory, but it seems to work.

The recipe for potato-cheese soup fits my criteria both for food and for the symbolism of food. It's warm, filling and cosy, which is how I want friends to feel in my home, and it's foolproof. You can double or diddle with the ingredients, but you cannot ruin it. I find this very relaxing, and my friends know that in an uncertain world, this soup is one thing that is utterly dependable; which I think is actually quite a lot for a meal to provide.

serves 6–8

2 cups/300g/11oz diced, peeled potatoes	
1 cup/175g/6oz chopped onion	
½ cup/50g/2oz diced celery	
2½ cups/600ml/1pt boiling water	
1 tsp salt	
¼ cup/50g/2oz butter or margarine	
¼ cup/50g/2oz flour	
2 tsp salt	
¼ tsp pepper	
½ tsp powdered mustard	
1½ tsp Worcester sauce	
2 cups/500ml/16fl oz milk	
2 cups/225g/8oz grated sharp (mature) Cheddar cheese	
1 cup/200g/7oz canned stewed tomatoes	

In a heavy kettle (pan), bring the first five ingredients to a boil, cover and simmer for 15 minutes.

In a large saucepan, melt the butter, add the flour, and cook/combine for a minute. Blend in the salt, pepper, mustard, Worcester sauce, and milk; then add the cheese and tomatoes. Cook, stirring, until smooth and thick.

Combine with the potato mixture and add the parsley. Simmer briefly and serve with salad and good rolls or bread.

Joan Barfoot is an internationally acclaimed Canadian novelist. Her début novel, *Gaining Ground* (The Women's Press, 1980), won the *Books in Canada* award for best first novel of the year when it was published there under the title *Abra*. Her other novels are *Dancing in the Dark* (1982), made into the award-winning film of the same name, *Duet for Three* (1986), *Family News* (1990), *Plain Jane* (1992) and *Charlotte and Claudia Keeping in Touch* (1994) — all published by The Women's Press. Joan Barfoot lives in London, Ontario.

Morue Raccommodé
(Pot Luck Codfish) MARYSE CONDÉ

'Only brainless women like to cook,' my mother was fond of reasoning. Day in, day out she was content to draw up the menus with Delia, our servant girl, then ration out the shopping money and send her off to market. Yet she had worshipped her own mother who, as long as she lived, had hired out her culinary services and every year in August had paraded in front of the cathedral of St Peter and St Paul with the insignia of the Patron Saint of Cooks embroidered on an apron around her hips.

Perhaps it was my mother's secret, mysterious way of mourning the distance that had grown between them ever since they had left the poverty of their rural home to come and live in town. In order to raise her, her mother had continued her thankless job from table to table while she had become the pride and joy of her teachers from school to school. In the end her mother died the year of her engagement to my father and was never to see her installed in an upstairs–downstairs house or the quick succession of christenings in silk and lace.

My mother only set foot in the kitchen on those rare occasions when Delia took a day off, and without exception cooked this recipe which is engraved in my memory.

serves 6

500g/18oz salted codfish
....
500g/18oz potatoes
....
4 plump tomatoes, chopped
....

3 cloves garlic, crushed

2 large onions, chopped

3 big red (bell) peppers, cored, deseeded and chopped

3 green (bell) peppers, cored, deseeded and chopped

chopped mint leaves

olive oil

salt (optional)

juice of 1 lemon

ground black pepper

hot pepper (optional)

1¼ cups/150g/5oz grated Gruyère cheese

Soak the codfish in cold water for 4–5 hours before cooking it in boiling water, then cut it up into large pieces. Boil the potatoes in their skins, making sure they stay firm, then cut into slices. In a blender or food processor, prepare a tomato purée heavily seasoned with garlic. In a frying pan, brown the onions, red and green peppers and chopped mint leaves in olive oil. When ready, mix in the tomato purée, adding salt (if necessary), lemon juice, ground pepper, and hot pepper if need be.

Preheat the oven at 350°F/180°C/Gas 4. In an oven-proof dish, make alternative layers of potatoes, codfish and sautéed pepper and tomato mixture. Top off by sprinkling with the grated Gruyère. If need be, add 2 tablespoons of olive oil. Bake for 35–40 minutes.

Maryse Condé is the award-winning author of *Segu*, *The Children of Segu* and *Tree of Life* (The Women's Press, 1994). A native of Guadeloupe, she lived for many years in Paris, where she taught Caribbean literature at the Sorbonne. She is the recipient of the prestigious Le Grand Prix Litteraire de la Femme, was a Guggenheim Fellow in 1987–88, and in 1993 was the first woman to be honoured as a Puterbaugh Fellow by the University of Oklahoma. She currently divides her time between the United States and Guadeloupe.

Grenadian Fish Cakes   JEAN BUFFONG

This dish is very popular in the Caribbean, in particular Grenada, and forms part of the breakfast-time meal. In addition to the fry-bakes or West Indian bread, the usual drink at breakfast will be a cup of cocoa (not from a tin but pure locally processed cocoa).

makes approximately 15 cakes

1 350g/12oz packet dried salt codfish
....
2 cups/225g/8oz plain (all-purpose) flour
....
cold water
....
vegetable oil for frying
....
fresh green or red hot peppers, cored, deseeded and finely chopped
....
fresh chives (if unavailable substitute spring onions), finely chopped
....
fresh thyme (if unavailable use dried thyme), finely chopped
....
1 large onion, finely chopped
....
ground black pepper
....

Soak the dried salt codfish in cold water (preferably overnight). Boil for about 15 minutes. Rinse, bone and crush.

Mix the flour with enough cold water to make a thick batter that just drops from the spoon. Add the onion, chives, thyme and hot pepper to the batter. Season with salt and black pepper and mix together thoroughly.

Add the dried salt codfish and mix again, making sure

that all the ingredients are evenly distributed. Leave to stand for about 1 hour.

Shallow fry dessertspoonfuls of the batter in sizzling hot oil. Turn occasionally until crispy and brown.

Serve hot or cold, ideally with Grenadian fry-bakes or West Indian bread.

Jean Buffong is a Grenadian novelist who has lived in England since 1962. Her novella, *Jump-Up-and-Kiss-Me*, was published by The Women's Press in 1990, and was followed by the novels *Under the Silk Cotton Tree* (The Women's Press, 1992) and *Snowflakes in the Sun* (The Women's Press, 1994).

Roast Breadfruit with Ackee and Salt Fish VERNELLA FULLER

My mother tells me that when I was a child I enjoyed eating a variety of food. One food though that I would not touch was breadfruit. This is a starchy vegetable marked by a distinctive prickly green skin. It is cream on the inside, has a breadlike texture and can be prepared in a variety of ways: it can be roasted with the skin left on, peeled and boiled, or boiled and then fried.

Apparently, my revulsion to breadfruit lay with the skin. As far back as she can remember, my mother says, the skin has caused me great discomfort. For some inexplicable reason, on seeing it, I would scratch my body furiously and demand that it be moved out of my sight. This was particularly inconvenient because breadfruit was one of the crops that grew liberally on my grandmother's property, where we lived, making it a staple part of our diet.

My mother tried preparing the breadfruit for me in many ways. She also tried making it seem as appetising as possible serving it with my favourite, steamed fish or with meat, with colourful mixed vegetables, with calaloo (of the spinach family) or ackee. She even tried disguising it, all to no avail. It seemed I could spot the breadfruit a mile off, whatever the disguise.

Then my parents left me for a week with a godmother. The childless, anxious woman, on taking all the instructions to ensure I was happy and did not miss home too much, was told specifically of my aversion to breadfruit.

But one of the first things she said to my mother on her return was, 'I thought you said V. does not like breadfruit? She's eaten nothing else since you left! I like it roasted, and was having it with a tip of salt on the first day she was here. She asked for some. Since then she's wanted it every day.' And to this day roast breadfruit with ackee and salt fish is my favourite dish.

I go to Jamaica once every two years now and this is always the first meal I ask my mother to prepare for me (although, thankfully, all the ingredients for this can be acquired in Britain today).

ACKEE AND SALT FISH

1 450g/1lb packet dried salt fish (preserved cod)

1 medium-size onion, sliced

1 red or green (bell) pepper, cored, deseeded and sliced

2 or 3 tomatoes, chopped, or 1 small can tomatoes

2 tbsp coconut oil (olive oil or sunflower oil will do)

1 can ackee (This tropical vegetable can be obtained from some large supermarkets or Asian and Caribbean shops.)

freshly ground black pepper

mixed herbs

dash of West Indian hot pepper sauce (optional)

Soak the salt fish in cold water overnight. Discard the water and bring the fish to the boil in fresh water. You may wish to discard the water again and boil a second time or even a third time if fish is still too salty for your taste. Leave the fish to cool, then remove the skin and bones.

Fry the onion and red or green pepper together in the oil (I like these to be crunchy). Add the salt fish and fry for a few minutes. Add the chopped tomatoes and cook for a few more minutes.

Add the ackee; this is already cooked so only needs to be heated through. Season with freshly ground black pepper and mixed herbs. Add hot pepper sauce to taste.

While preparing the Ackee and Salt Fish, you can start cooking the Roast Breadfruit.

ROAST BREADFRUIT

Preheat the oven to 160°C/300°F/Gas 2. Place the breadfruit (450–900g/1–2lb) in its skin on the middle shelf. Allow 30 minutes for each 450g/1lb. After the allotted time, pierce the breadfruit with a knife. The knife should come away clean. If not, allow another 15 minutes at 100°C/200°F/Gas ¼.

An even better way of roasting breadfruit in the skin is to barbecue it. The aroma is fantastic and the texture and taste are better than one that has been conventionally oven-roasted. This is the traditional method of cooking in rural Jamaica.

When roasted, remove the skin and cut into slices.

Serve with ackee and salt fish and mixed green salad.

Vernella Fuller was born in St Catherine, Jamaica, in 1956. At the age of twelve, she moved to England to join her parents. She now lives in Sutton with her daughter, Alisha. Vernella Fuller is the author of the novels, *Going Back Home* (1992) and *Unlike Normal Women* (1995), both published by The Women's Press.

Good Look Food (for uncertain cooks) STEPHANIE DOWRICK

Whatever else may be memorable about my company, it is not my cooking.

The high point of My Life as a Cook may well be when my desire to persuade my two infant children to eat a little more than mouse portions led me to create flagrantly enticing pictures from food on their large white plates. A carrot nose to rival Pinocchio's; knobbly sultana ears; abundant bleach-blonde cottage cheese hair; a sprightly sprig of parsley for a bow; a widely smiling red capsicum (pepper) mouth; none of it was too much trouble for me, perhaps because creating such pictures also tempered the uncomfortable mixture of boredom and pessimistic insecurity that too often strikes me as I enter a kitchen.

My ideal meal still ranks aesthetics higher than cooking skills. Good Look principles can be widely applied. The meal that follows is just an example and what passes for a recipe will be needed only by new or timid cooks. It displays and offers food that ranges in colour from palest pink to nutty brown with several shades and shapes of green. Platters and plates also matter. They need to be large in size and number. A *laden* table is a very good look.

An apology: This particular meal is best bought and prepared in Australia where food is brilliantly fresh, varied and still affordable. For those who need to, happy travelling!

optional salad ingredients: avocado/red pepper/white spring onions/baby tomatoes/fresh coriander (cilantro), according to your mood and pocket

new potatoes (lots)

mushrooms (lots)

Chinese greens – bok choy or one of its cousins (heaps as they cook down fast)

extra virgin olive oil

optional: black olives, fresh basil, pesto, anchovies, chillies, pine nuts, *very* expensive bought mayonnaise for the fish

butter

salt and freshly ground black pepper

fresh asparagus (lots)

fat fresh tuna steaks (or salmon steaks, but definitely NOT meat. In the absence of such ideal fish, stick to the vegetables only and tart up the potatoes with lots of pine nuts. The meal will still be terrific.)

Soy or teriaki sauce

Clean and arrange the raw vegetables. Don't think 'salad'. Think 'still-life'.

Cook the washed and unpeeled potatoes. When the skins begin to split, they are probably ready. Poke them to find out. Turn them off just as they're ready, then let them steam away in the small amount of water that's left for at least 5 more minutes while you wipe the mushrooms clean and wash the Chinese greens in several changes of water.

Drain and tip the potatoes into a big bowl in which already lies enough excellent olive oil to cover them lightly – and something else. This could be black olives chopped finely *or* fresh basil *or* some ready-prepared pesto sauce *or* tiny pieces of cut-up anchovies *or* strips of roasted red pepper *or* possibly some chillies if that's to your taste *or* lots of pine nuts which you may want to dry-roast briefly to brown them and increase their flavour. Cover all the potatoes with the olive oil mixture. Leave them to sit. The longer, the better.

Thickly cut the mushrooms if large. Shut them up in a smallish saucepan with a knob of butter, black pepper and possibly some basil or coriander – even dried would do. Turn them over from time to time. Five minutes on low heat is enough. Turn off the heat before they are quite ready so they can sit while you are still running. When it's time to eat, tip them into a bowl that harbours their juice.

The asparagus is tricky to cook without a steamer, but worth it. Prop the stalks up in fast-boiling water. The tips will steam while the bottoms boil. After about 5 minutes check they are tender, then stop the cooking by draining them and running cold water over them for a second. If you have enough, flaunt them on their own flat dish. If not, let them wait to be tall green warriors standing by the fish. Dribble butter over them if you must.

Tackle the fish and the Chinese greens together.

The fish can be cooked under a medium-hot grill (broiler) or on a barbecue. It should only take about 4 minutes each side. Don't do anything to it but brush it with oil and gratitude.

Chinese greens are best stir-fried in a hot wok with a dash of olive oil. Once they are in, add a little water, and as much soy or teriaki sauce as you like. Make sure they are grit-free and throw in the chopped white stems first. Follow with the torn leaves which will wilt in seconds. Stir-frying may seem a bit much with one eye on the grill, but 3–4 minutes are all that's needed. Bring the greens in the wok to the table, placing it on a wooden board and adding a handsome ladle for serving.

The colours are wonderful in this meal; the combination of moist flavours is even better. If you can trust the ingredients and pay close attention for no more than 30 minutes, it is impossible to ruin. I promise.

Stephanie Dowrick was born in New Zealand, lived in Europe for much of her adult life, and now lives with her children in Sydney, Australia. She works as a writer and psychotherapist, and among her books are *Running Backwards Over Sand* the international bestseller, *Intimacy and Solitude* (The Women's Press, 1992); and *The Intimacy and Solitude Self-Therapy Book* (The Women's Press, 1993). She co-founded The Women's Press, was Managing Director from 1977 to 1982, and is currently its Chairwoman.

Chicken with Tarragon, Leaf Spinach and Cream Potatoes with Lemon and Dill ANGELA NEUSTATTER

I created the chicken and spinach dish as a way of persuading my then young sons, both of whom seemed convinced that vegetables would damage their health, to eat spinach. Once it was mixed in with the cream and chicken, they saw it as something different. I first ate the dill and potato dish while attending a writing course on the Greek island of Skyros. At the end of one particularly gruelling day when the Muse had resolutely refused to visit and I was feeling very despondent, this utterly delicious dish with its sharp, rich flavour was served and it was indeed food for the soul. I ate far more than was good for me and went home and wrote most of the night!

I find the combination of these two dishes quite delicious and they have the virtue of being simple and quick to prepare and it's been much appreciated at many a dinner party.

serves 6

CHICKEN AND TARRAGON WITH LEAF SPINACH

6 boned breasts of chicken

medium bunch of fresh tarragon

3 tbsp olive oil

675g/1½lb fresh spinach or equivalent pack of frozen leaf spinach

2½ cups/1pt/600ml single (light) cream

salt and pepper

Wrap the chicken breasts in silver foil and slow cook in low oven (approximately 180°C/350°F/Gas 4) until just cooked right through. Chop the tarragon and fry for 1 minute in the olive oil. Add the chicken breasts and toss them in the oil and tarragon mixture for 2 minutes, then remove the pan from the heat. Cook the fresh spinach or defrost and warm the frozen spinach. Add to the chicken and tarragon mixture and pour on the cream. Return to the heat and stir together very thoroughly. Add salt and pepper to taste. Put in an ovenproof dish and cook for 20 minutes in the oven at a low heat (approximately 180°C/350°F/Gas 4).

POTATOES WITH LEMON AND DILL

1.20kg/2½lb potatoes with a slightly soft texture (Cyprus potatoes or salad potatoes are ideal)

2 large onions

5 tbsp olive oil

50g/2oz butter

a large bunch of dill

2 lemons

salt and pepper

Peel the potatoes, boil them until cooked and chop into medium-sized chunks. Peel and chop the onion. Heat the olive oil and butter in a very large frying pan. Add the onion and cook until soft but not brown. Add the dill and cook for 1 minute. Add the potatoes and cook for 10 minutes, turning the mixture over regularly to prevent it burning. Squeeze the lemons and pour the juice in with potatoes. Add salt and pepper to taste.

Angela Neustatter is a freelance journalist, writing for the *Guardian, Independent, Telegraph Magazine* and *You Maga-*

zine. She also co-edits a magazine for Unicef. She is the author of six books, the most recent being *Look the Demon in the Eye — The Challenge of Mid-life* (Michael Joseph). She lives in North London with her partner and two sons.

Apple and Shallot Relish
HELEN DUNMORE

After years of daily cooking for children, I'm hungry for meals cooked by other people. At my parents' house, my father cooks for me. He has always loved to cook fish and shellfish, and I remember from childhood big pans of steaming mussels, the bloody gutting of mackerel, and crabs with the sweetest meat in their claws. We had a stainless steel claw-cracker, and picks to dig out the white crab-flesh. But these were holiday dishes, while my mother cooked daily for six until her pleasure in cooking was doused by repetition. So now my father cooks for her every evening. When we visit, he feeds the grandchildren first, then the adults sit and eat perhaps a piece of fresh cod with butter or wine sauce, or baked mullet, or salmon which has been cooling in its silver foil on the kitchen balcony which overlooks the sea.

I shop weekly in a supermarket, and while I always like buying food, it's not very interesting to have to keep in mind who will eat this and who won't eat that. Too often the result is compromise food, not the food I really want to cook. The meals mustn't take too long to prepare, and must be more or less liked by everyone. There's something a bit arid and repetitive about it, and I know exactly why my mother stopped wanting to cook. But now my parents have finished with supermarkets, and they shop daily, thoughtfully and with pleasure. Their cod comes from a local catch, their plums and apples from a farm. Their sausages are a loose, meaty coil wrapped in white paper. Here is a relish my father makes, which goes well with a robust fish such as mackerel, or with pan-fried pork steaks.

3–4 shallots
3 apples (they should be firm; so they do not disintegrate in cooking, and full-flavoured – Cox's or Jonagold would be fine.)
1 tbsp light oil, such as grapeseed (or you could use butter)
1 tbsp clear honey
about 1 wineglass dry cider
freshly ground black pepper

Slice the shallots and cut the apples into pieces. Add the shallots to the oil in a heavy saucepan and cook gently until soft. Add the apples, honey, cider and black pepper. Cook over a low heat with a tight-fitting lid until the apples are soft but not mushy.

If there is too much liquid, pour some off and reduce, then add to the remaining relish. Serve the relish with fish or pork. It can also be served cold with cold meat.

Helen Dunmore has published fiction for both adults and children, as well as six collections of poetry. Prizes and awards for her work include the Signal Poetry Award, the Poetry Society's Alice Hunt Bartlett Award, and the McKitterick Prize for her first novel, *Zennor in Darkness*. She received the Orange Prize for fiction for her third novel, *A Spell of Winter*.

Irish Stew MAEVE BINCHY

I'm not a great cook but when my English husband, Gordon Snell, and I bought a house in Ireland, he was very ignorant of Irish food. I wasn't much help to him and he said if only the recipes were in verse, he'd remember them. But there wasn't a rhyming Irish cookbook so he wrote one!

It was great for me because he is meticulous and honest and tried out all the recipes. Often people think Irish Stew is bones and a bit dull, but if you have nice lean chops and lots of flavours, it's just gorgeous.

serves 6–8

1kg/2¼lb boned mutton or stewing lamb
....
4 large potatoes
....
2 large onions
....
1 turnip
....
2 stalks celery
....
barley
....
thyme and parsley
....
salt and pepper
....

> For Irish Stew, remember that
> It's best to trim the meat of fat.
> Your onions and potatoes slice
> And celery and turnips dice.

Now take a casserole and place
Some vegetables in the base.
Then add some meat, cut into squares,
And so on, in alternate layers.

There's many a cook in Ireland who
Will add a little barley too;
At this stage, sprinkle if you wish
Herbs, salt and pepper on the dish.

Add water, boil it up, then stop
And skim the fat from off the top.
Now three hours simmering should do
To make a tender Irish Stew.

(From *The Rhyming Irish Cookbook* by Gordon Snell
(published by The O'Brien Press, Dublin, 1992)

Maeve Binchy is the author of the bestselling novels, *Light a Penny Candle*, *Echoes*, *Circle of Friends*, *Copper Beech*, *The Glass Lake* and *Evening Class*. She was born in Dalkey, Co Dublin and worked as a columnist for the *Irish Times*.

Baked Chicken Pilaf MARGE PIERCY

You might call this dish Chicken Diana, because my friend Diana der Hovanessian often does Armenian cooking for me when we have lunch. This is my attempt at something like what she cooks, my homage to her cooking. We meet a couple of times a month when we can and show each other our recent work. Diana is a poet and a translator from the Armenian. She has also published translations from the Russian and the Roumanian. We met perhaps ten years ago when the New England Poetry Club was sponsoring me for a reading. She is now their president. I often find that knowing I am about to see Diana causes me to finish poems that have been languishing incomplete or roughly done.

serves about 6

1–2 cups/175–350g/6–12 oz white or brown rice
....
chicken stock or dissolve a chicken bouillon (stock) cube
....
olive oil
....
allspice
....
powdered cinnamon
....
1 chicken, cut into pieces (you can remove the skin or not, as you please)
....
2 jars or cans of tomatoes (or use fresh, skinned tomatoes)
....
a little white wine or vermouth
....
fresh mushrooms (optional)
....

Preheat the oven to 160°C/325°F/Gas 3.

In a saucepan, boil however much rice you want in chicken stock and partially cook it.

Brown the chicken pieces for 10 minutes on each side, preferably in olive oil. Add allspice and cinnamon.

Grease a casserole. Put in the chicken pieces, rice and any remaining stock, tomatoes, more spices, a little white wine or vermouth. Cover the casserole and cook for 40 minutes or so. Very good, but watch it doesn't dry out.

You can sauté some mushrooms briefly and add them for the last 20 minutes of baking. This is optional.

Note: This recipe lends itself to many variations in the spicing. You could go for herbs instead of spices: Oregano, thyme, and tarragon or basil would work very well. You could add red wine instead of white.

Marge Piercy is an internationally acclaimed author and poet. Her bestselling books include *Woman on the Edge of Time* (The Women's Press, 1979), *The High Cost of Living* (The Women's Press, 1979), *Vida* (The Women's Press, 1980), *Summer People, Fly Away Home, Gone to The Soldiers, Body of Glass* (winner of the Arthur C Clarke Award for Best Science Fiction), *The Longings of Women* and *The Eight Chambers of the Heart* (a selection of poetry). Her latest novel, *City of Darkness, City of Light*, is published by Michael Joseph in 1997.

Chicken with a Little Help from My Friends MARCIA MULLER

The original version of this recipe was concocted over a dozen years ago, when I was newly single and wanted to thank my friends for the many favors they had done me during a difficult year. I planned to accomplish this with a series of dinner parties and, since I was unaccustomed to entertaining alone, decided I could manage best if I had one basic, easy menu. For a seemingly endless number of weekends I served this chicken dish with pasta and a green salad – becoming thoroughly sick of it and determined never to eat it again.

The recipe stood me in good stead, however, and a few years later I had a character in one of my novels prepare it. Upon the book's publication, suggestions began to arrive. Chuck and Marianne in Connecticut wrote to say they'd prepared it, adding a dash of white pepper. Jan in Texas threw in a quarter teaspoon of Worcestershire sauce. Suzanne in Los Angeles was horrified that I had sautéed the chicken in the liquid from the marinated mushrooms; use olive oil, for heaven's sake, she said. Anne in Fort Wayne, Indiana, told me to lose the marinated mushrooms and use fresh ones. Hank in Florida suggested I steam fresh artichokes and quarter their hearts, rather than use the canned version; he did admit that he was retired and had time for such activities, and I took that as permission not to follow his advice. A reader who shall remain nameless confessed to introducing sun-dried tomatoes, prompting her son to exclaim, 'Yuck! This stuff is *awful!*'

A few years ago I decided I had sufficiently recovered from my overdose of this dish and prepared it again, taking into account all the reader suggestions. Here, in final form, is the creation of many cooks.

serves 4

1 tbsp extra virgin olive oil

2 cloves garlic, minced

225g/8oz small fresh mushrooms

6 boneless, skinless chicken breasts

1 large can pitted ripe olives

1 large can quartered artichoke hearts

$1/4$ tsp Worcestershire sauce

$1/2$ tsp oregano

a dash of white pepper

$1/4$ cup/60ml/2fl oz dry white wine

a few sprigs of fresh rosemary

shredded Parmesan cheese

Heat the olive oil to a medium-high temperature and sauté the minced garlic for 2 minutes. Add the fresh mushrooms and sauté for 2 minutes more. Remove. (You may have to add more olive oil at this point – that's up to the individual cook.) Brown the chicken breasts over a medium-high heat. Transfer, along with garlic and mushrooms, to a casserole. Top with the olives and artichoke hearts.

In a pan, heat the Worcestershire sauce, oregano, white pepper, and white wine over a medium heat. Pour over the contents of the casserole. Top with rosemary sprigs and Parmesan cheese to taste. Bake in a preheated oven at 180°C/350°F/Gas 4 until the chicken is fully cooked and the cheese has melted.

Serve with pasta and garden salad – but not ten times in a row!

Marcia Muller created the first-ever hardboiled female private eye with the first Sharon McCone mystery, *Edwin of the Iron Shoes*. Her Sharon McCone mysteries are now major international bestsellers, and include *Ask the Cards a Question*, *Games to Keep the Dark Away*, *Leave a Message for Willie*, *There's Something in a Sunday*, *The Shape of Dread*, *Trophies and Dead Things*, *Where Echoes Live*, *Pennies on a Dead Woman's Eyes*, *Wolf in the Shadows*, *Till the Butchers Cut Him Down* and *The Broken Promise Land* – all published by The Women's Press. She has been nominated for the Edgar Allan Poe Award for Best Crime Novel, the Shamus Award, and has won the Anthony Boucher Award for Best Novel of the Year. In 1993, Marcia Muller was awarded the Private Eye Writers of America Life Achievement Award.

Beltane Bake CAEIA MARCH

Our women's group here in Cornwall has a wonderful time during our festival of the Eve of Summer. We do ritual together eight times a year – the solstices, equinoxes and the Celtic cross quarter days: Imbolc, Beltane, Lughnasad and Samhain.

We begin our Beltane festival with a celebration ritual somewhere on the moors at a stone circle or dolmen, starting at sunset on the night before May Day. Traditionally the Celtic day starts and finishes at sunset. Beltane is a fire festival, derived from the Irish words *Bel Teine* – meaning Good Fire. We give thanks for the summer to come and ask for fertility for ourselves and the earth. Our fertility doesn't have to mean having babies. We might be creating a new book, painting, sculpture, series of photographs or handcrafts, new friendships, gardens, lover relationships, and delight in one another. We leap over our Beltane fire in ones and twos to symbolise the passion and fusion of this creativity and the leaving behind of all that which we wish to discard.

After the ritual we have a wonderful Beltane feast where we all bring food and wine to share. If the evening is too chilly, we return to one of our homes for our feast and then we drum and dance for a long time and tell stories and make merry.

On May Day itself our group drives up to Padstow for one of the few remaining folk festivals in Britain. This time we celebrate without our drums which would be intrusive there. We're in the crowd who follow the Obby Oss through the decorated streets for May Day. The Oss has its origins in Mare, Goddess of the Sea (who resembles the Celtic horse goddess, Epona). These days, however, the Mare has become a male Oss, a reversion of the original meaning.

A wonderful atmosphere and an ancient eerie drum beat, like a heart beat, fills the air between the granite terraces of fishing folk's houses there. Everyone is smiling – a Cornish carnival dating from pre-Christian times. We buy marzipan and ice creams. We return home weary but happy, passing through lanes lined with May blossom and white with native three-cornered leeks. A simply delicious free food, and so called because the cross section of the stem is triangular which makes them distinctive in appearance, the heralds of summer here in the south-west of England.

serves 8

1 large Spanish onion, finely chopped

vegetable oil or Fry Light

1¼ cups/200g/7oz mixed dried beans, soaked overnight and boiled until edible

1 cup/15g/4oz cup grated vegetarian cheese

one colander full of washed chopped stems and leaves of the three-cornered leeks, which grow wild in the Cornish countryside and in Cornish gardens in April and May

fresh herbs

2 cups full of flower heads of three-cornered leeks, washed

Sauté the chopped onion in a small amount of vegetable oil or Fry Light, if preferred. Mix together in a large bowl all the ingredients except the white flower heads. Add fresh herbs to taste – we use fresh oregano and a very tiny amount of fresh sage.

Put the mixture in an ovenproof dish without a lid, and

bake in a preheated oven at 180°C/350°F/Gas 4 for about 45 minutes.

Serve hot or cold, decorated with the flowers which are edible and very pretty. They look like a cross between snowdrops and white bluebells!

Note: If shop-bought leeks are substituted, please add a clove of (chopped) garlic to your bake.

Caeia March grew up in industrial South Yorkshire and now lives in Cornwall where she is a countrywoman and keen gardener. She is a founder member and one of the trustees of the West Cornwall Women's Land Trust. She is an enthusiastic vegetarian cook and loves to make unusual birthday cakes, a talent which she developed when her sons were young. Caeia March is also the author of *Three Ply Yarn* (1986), *The Hide and Seek Files* (1988), *Fire! Fire!* (1990), *Reflections* (1995) and *Between the Worlds* (1996) – all published by The Women's Press.

74

Tomato Sauce #1 with Pasta
JOYCE CAROL OATES

It was a gusty, snow-swirling night; we'd driven for many hours from upstate New York to arrive more than an hour late for dinner at the home of our dear friends Jeannie and Dan Halpern, who live in a semi-rural area of Princeton, New Jersey; we'd seen an excellent but emotionally draining production of my play *I Stand Before You Naked* (a play for ten women), and were both exhausted; we arrived quite literally in a blizzardy blast, and within minutes were made to feel warm, welcome, cheered up and in every way enlivened by the presence of the Halperns and their two-year-old daughter Lily (who used to sleep in a tiny cradle on the dining room table as an infant, at our 'family dinners at the Halperns' only a brief while ago). This elegant, delicious, yet relatively 'simple' recipe was our dinner that night; I recommend it for cold, blustery winter nights when the soul is in need of companionable nourishment. (With grateful acknowledgment to Jeannie and Daniel Halpern.)

serves 4

3 tbsp olive oil

1 large Spanish onion, quartered lengthwise and sliced

2 carrots, chopped

2 stalks celery, chopped

1/2 tsp red pepper flakes (more or less, to taste)

1 tbsp oregano

1 tbsp dried mint

1 tbsp dried celery leaves

1 bay leaf

salt and pepper to taste

6 cloves garlic, minced

$1/4$ dried tomatoes, minced (sold in this form)

$1/4$ cup/60ml/2fl oz red wine

$1/4$ cup/60ml/2fl oz marsala

3 tbsp balsamic vinegar

1l/35 oz/$1^3/_4$pt can tomato purée

450g/1 lb *rotelle* (wheel-shaped pasta) or other pasta shape

In a large casserole, heat the oil and add the onion, carrots, celery, red pepper flakes, oregano, mint, celery leaves, bay leaf, and salt and pepper to taste. Cook until the vegetables are soft.

Add the garlic and cook for another 2 minutes. Add the red wine, marsala, and vinegar, and cook for a minute or two at a boil, to reduce the liquid slightly. Stir in the tomato purée and mix well. Bring to a boil, lower the heat, and simmer, covered, for 30–60 minutes.

Prepare the pasta and add it to the sauce. Stir well and serve immediately, with Parmesan on the side.

Joyce Carol Oates is the author most recently of the novel, *What I Lived For*. She is a regular contributor to the *Times Literary Supplement* and is on the faculty of Princeton University.

Smoked Aubergine Pasta
VAL McDERMID

Food and love have always been woven together in my heart. When I was born, I was suspected of having TB and kept in an infectious diseases hospital thirty miles away from my parents. They had no car, and there was no public transport link between the two places. So for the first six weeks of my life, the only time I was cuddled was when I was fed. Now, feeding my friends is one of the strongest ways I have of telling them I love them. I enjoy cooking, and there's nothing beats an evening round a table with people I care about and good food.

I learned this recipe on holiday in Spain with my partner and an ever-shifting group of friends. While she was scuba diving, my new friend Perran the chef and I were sweating in the kitchen, sharing recipes and laughter. I've since cooked it many times for celebrations with friends, and it's always a winner.

serves 4

1 large aubergine (eggplant)

2 red (bell) peppers

1 onion

1 tbsp olive oil

1 large handful of fresh basil

1 400g/14oz can tomatoes

1 tin tomato concentrate

1 400g/14oz can black olives

black pepper

2 tbsp caramelised onions

FOR CARAMELISED ONIONS:

2 tbsp olive oil or 1 tbsp each of oil and butter

900g/2lb onions, coarsely chopped

2 tbsp brown sugar

3 tbsp water

1 tbsp balsamic vinegar to deglaze

Pasta shapes for four (fresh is best, dried will do)

First, start the caramelised onions. Heat the oil in a heavy bottomed pan, then add the coarsely chopped onions, the sugar and the water. Cook slowly over a low heat until the onions are soft and starting to go brown and the liquid has boiled down to a sticky brown residue. Add the vinegar and stir briskly for a few minutes, allowing a little of the vinegar to boil off. When cool, the onions can be kept for up to a month in the refrigerator and added to pasta sauces, pizza toppings or used as a pickle with cheese.

While the onions are cooking, the aubergines and peppers have their first cooking. Either on a barbecue, over a high gas flame, or under a hot grill (broiler), they must be flamed until the skin is black and cracking. Once they are completely blackened, place them in a bowl and cover it so that juices escaping in the form of steam are not lost. When the vegetables are cooled, scrape off the skin with the back of a knife. Dice the aubergine and core and slice the peppers.

Chop the onion finely and cook it gently in the olive oil over a medium heat until it softens. Add the diced aubergine and the sliced peppers and cook for a few minutes, stirring constantly. Roughly chop or tear the basil and add it with the canned tomatoes, the tomato concentrate, the drained olives, half the caramelised onions and a grinding of black pepper. Add the strained juices from the cooling aubergine and peppers. Simmer for 20 minutes. Before serving with pasta shapes, stir in the remaining caramelised onions.

Leftover tip: If there are any leftovers (unlikely!) this is great eaten cold with a teaspoonful of mayonnaise stirred in.

Val McDermid grew up in a Scottish mining community and worked as a journalist for several years, before becoming a full-time novelist. She is the bestselling author of the Kate Brannigan mystery series and the Lindsay Gordon mystery series which includes the novels, *Report for Murder* (1987), *Common Murder* (1989), *Final Edition* (1991), *Union Jack* (1993) and *Booked for Murder* (1996) – all published by The Women's Press. Val McDermid won the Crime Writers' Association Gold Dagger Award for best crime novel in 1995.

Pasta Putanesca JOANNA BRISCOE

Puttanesca is a recent and rapturous find. It reminds me of a particular summer, of shivering, drunk and drowsy at one in the morning on Primrose Hill, of my friend Diane Gray-Smith, and of my cousin Eleanor. Though I shudder at its name, it's perversely appropriate. The hot, hot summer of '95 infected me with a sudden barking madness, as though discovering adolescence again. I could hardly write, I had three abrupt flirtations, one affair, and more wine and Pimms and Puttanesca than I had ever thought likely. Diane made the pasta one night. I'm a bored and whining cook, but this was fun, and I stole the recipe for my repertoire, turned my cousin into a rabid addict, and flirted with a particular actress over the olives. I've been gripped ever since.

serves 2

1 onion, finely chopped
....
olive oil
....
2 cloves garlic, crushed
....
1 400g/14oz can tomatoes
....
squirt of tomato purée (paste)
....
2 fresh green chillies, finely chopped
....
3 tbsp capers
....
1 85g/3oz can (approximately) anchovies, chopped
....
a little over 1 cup/115g/4oz of pitted black olives
....
pasta, preferably penne tricolore
....

Gently cook the onion in olive oil in a heavy pan, and add the crushed garlic. Add the tomatoes, including the juice, with a squirt or two of tomato purée and the chillies (according to taste). Mash the tomatoes a little, mix, and simmer for about 20 minutes, until the sauce is thick and fairly solid, with a consistency like marmalade. Add the capers, chopped anchovies including a little of their oil, and a mixture of halved and whole olives. Simmer very gently for another 10 minutes.

Simply serve a couple of spoonfuls on top of the pasta, preferably penne tricolore, without mixing in the sauce. Eat with fresh Parmesan, a leaf salad, some red wine and a hot crusty loaf of ciabatta or focaccia.

This is a very hot, very rich sauce – its name disconcertingly meaning 'whorish' – and is delicious with even more chilli. Serve only small portions, the penne tasting clean and cool in contrast to the sauce.

Joanna Briscoe was born in London in 1963. Her first novel, *Mothers and Other Lovers*, in which a mother-daughter relationship is echoed by the daughter's affair with an older woman, won the Betty Trask Award and was published by Phoenix House in 1994. Her second novel, *Skin* (Phoenix House, 1997) examines beauty and narcissism. She has published short stories in anthologies, including *School Tales* (Livewire Books, The Women's Press, 1990) and *Revenge* (Virago). She has also written for the *Guardian*, *Sunday Times*, *Observer*, *Sunday Independent*, *Evening Standard* and *Elle*. She lives in Bloomsbury, London, but spends a lot of time writing in New York.

Love Bites (Spicy Prawns)
YASMIN ALIBHAI-BROWN

It was the prawns (he says) that did it. And the movements of my small hands as I made him thin, flaky chappatis on a warm summer evening. In boring old Ealing. We were exhilarated, talking like we had known each other over many lifetimes, but had simply not met and there was all this catching up to do. He had drifted for years, with lovers who meant a lot but somehow something made commitment difficult. I had just watched the man who was my best friend, lover and father of my only child walk away with a young woman. After seventeen years. I was wounded, demented with pain, and starving for love and food. I lost more weight over those weeks than all those painful years of dieting and trying to rediscover that elusive waistline. This was the first evening in months I wanted to eat again, and even more miraculously to cook again. And I did. And I did not cry.

He watched me with his wide blue eyes, saying banal things at first about how he loved Indian food. Then as he fell in love with the smells and me – it took forty-five minutes – he started talking about a life together, the way he felt he had arrived home. We went to bed. And in spite of the wickedness of men, I believed him. Eight years on, the prawns still work their magic; we have a beautiful baby daughter, born when her mother was forty-five. He still says he loves me as much as he did that day. And that he always will. I am not fool enough to trust that last remark, even though I know that no one, but no one, can make spicy prawns and chappatis like I can.

serves 2

Approximately 4 cups/500g/16oz frozen prawns (shrimp) cheap or expensive, depending on how rich you're feeling.

small can tomato purée (paste)

1 tsp each of crushed garlic, ginger and coriander

1/2 tsp each of turmeric, crushed green chillis, ground coriander and ground cumin

juice of 1/2 lime

salt

2 tbsp oil

3 tbsp crème fraîche

Defrost the prawns and let them drain. Mix all the other ingredients except the crème fraîche in a blender. Marinate the prawns in the tomato and spice mixture for 30 minutes.

In a wok, heat the oil and stir-fry the prawns for 10–15 minutes. Stir in the crème fraîche.

Serve with chappatis. (If it is all right, I will hang on to that recipe for now.)

Yasmin Alibhai-Brown is the mother of an 18-year-old and three-year-old. She works as a freelance journalist and broadcaster, with a special interest in race and culture. She is the author of *No Place Like Home* and co-author of *The Colour of Love*.

'Falling in loff again, dahlink!'
(a meal of seduction)
FIONA COOPER

I call this menu 'Falling in loff again, dahlink!', because I did and so did she and, thank God and all the angels, we still are. She was knocked out by the food and by me, and has been heard to refer to it with nostalgia, as we are both too busy to do much more than beans on toast or take-aways these days. It marked the start of something wonderful for me, and I hope it does the same for you.

For this recipe to work, and for you to be bothered to work enough to do it, you need the following ingredients:
One: a shimmering pool of desire aimed at someone worth doing it for – it's the food of temptation, luxury and seduction. And Love.
Two: a day to shop and cook, unless you're one of these irritatingly organised people whose cupboards never get anywhere close to Mother Hubbard stage.
Three: a date with One, the day after Two. Choose a Friday or Saturday, and for God's sake have clean sheets. Break the habits of a lifetime and tidy and vacuum your entire flat. Conceal all dirty washing! You're out to impress!

This is your shopping list.

ATMOSPHERE: ELECTRIC
Fresh flowers – freesia, stargazer lilies, anything sweet smelling
2 bottles of pink champagne – or as near as you can afford
2 fluty glasses, if you have any
Greek brandy – 7–star metaxa
Canned strawberries or raspberries

Candles (soothing and seductive)
A mango — they're ripe when they smell like heaven

STARTERS: SEAFOOD IS SEXY

Can of anchovies
Prawns
Jar of fake caviar — red
4 fresh limes
Sour cream

SALAD: GREEN IS GORGEOUS

An avocado
Watercress
A mix of salad leaves. Break the bank at your supermarket if they do a pre-washed selection — if you buy five kinds of lettuce, you're eating it for days
Sunflower seeds, sesame seeds, flaked almonds, cashews, hazelnuts
Fab vinaigrette — raspberry is a wow

RED DRAGON PIE: RED IS RAMPANT

Red potatoes — about a pound
Can of chopped tomatoes
Can of tomato juice
Can of kidney beans
Red lentils
3 beef tomatoes
A red pepper
3 red onions
Tube or little can of tomato paste
2 carrots
Tube of garlic paste
Parmesan cheese
Soy sauce
Sesame oil
Oyster or brown cap mushrooms

Get this lot the day before the date. Go home and reward yourself with a glass of Greek brandy. Decide what you're going to wear. Check that it's clean. Hang it by an open window and don't change your mind. Put your favourite shampoo and bath oils by the bath. Are your towels clean? Is your toothpaste respectable? Is the champagne in the fridge? Go to sleep, if you can.

Start the cooking day about midday. Wear old clothes. Boring bits first: scrub the potatoes; float the salad leaves in a bowl of water; open the cans; wash and chop the peppers (small brick shapes) and carrots (batons); peel and chop the onions (half circles); scald the tomatoes and peel them and chop them into chunks; slice the oyster mushrooms in halves, except for two; dry-roast the sunflower seeds, nuts, etc (not the sesame seeds) until golden brown – shooshing them around a frying pan does fine – keep them separate, and bash half the hazelnuts to bits; have a small brandy; play your favourite music throughout – for me, it's Millie Jackson, Fats Waller and Liberace.

For the red dragon pie, you need a casserole. I bought one with exotic flowers on for the date which led to True Love. Chop the potatoes – unpeeled – into bite-sized bits and boil them for ten minutes. Then fry them very slightly in sesame oil and sesame seeds – then put to one side to use later. Put the peppers, carrots, onions, mushrooms, tomatoes, kidney beans into the casserole, mixing them all up. Add the cans of tomato and tomato juice. The mixture should look as damp and luscious as you feel. Put the casserole in a hot oven, covered, and leave it until it's bubbling. Then turn it down to simmer. Change the tape and have another drink. It's probably about three o'clock by now, so don't panic.

For the starter, I use glass shell-shaped plates. They're very camp. I also have gold plastic shell mats – even camper. Put a heap of prawns, a heap of fake caviar, and half the anchovies on each plate, arranged suggestively, leaving space for a sprig of watercress, an uncut mushroom, and a piece of frilly red lettuce, which go on at the last minute. Mix the sour cream with the juice of one lime and put it all into the fridge, covered.

Salad – a glass bowl for this. Put the leaves in, add the roasted sunflower seeds and cashews, toss it around a bit. The avocado goes in at the last minute or it goes brown. The vinaigrette stays in the bottle, or maybe a nice small jug, if you have one.

Look at the red dragon pie at about five o'clock. Cover the bean mixture with the potatoes and scatter hazelnuts, bashed and unbashed, on top. Sprinkle with Parmesan cheese and put it back in the oven, still on low.

Blend the can of raspberries or strawberries to a pulp, add three squeezed limes – not the peel, idiot! – and pour it into a glass jug which you then put in the fridge. Clean up the kitchen. Now you've done the messy bits, go and have a bath, do your hair and get dressed. Tell yourself you look lovely. Try and believe it!

It should be about six thirty now. Put the salad and mushroom bits on the starter plates. Cube the avocado and toss it through the salad. Play music that makes you feel witty and irresistible – avoid Abba, Tracy Chapman and Frank Sinatra. Your date doesn't need to know you are a trashy manic depressive slush bucket the minute she arrives. Place candles strategically and light them five minutes before you're expecting Her.

Speaking of which . . .

When the doorbell rings, *walk* to the front door, don't run. Act nonchalant – a warm smile is better than a wolfish leer. She is not – yet – close enough to hear your heartbeat! Ask her to pick some music and open the champagne while she's searching. Tip: for champagne, remove wire, take hold of cork in a tea-towel and twist gently. When you feel the cork pulse against your palm, hold it there, and *be near* the jug of crushed raspberries or strawberries. Pour in the entire bottle, and if you have a swizzle stick, then swizzle it now! A spoon will do. Pour out two glasses, replace the jug in the fridge and stroll towards Her. Engineer fingertip and eye contact as you give Her the glass. Sip and chat and refill. Let most of the jug be drunk before you eat.

Eat and enjoy, change tapes between courses. I recommend Errol Garner as the temperature rises, especially a long tape, or a CD which will replay. Tune into your rampant libidinous radar, and I hope you pick up as many signals as you're sending out. Before you jump on Her, try a lot of gentle contact – brushing Her beautiful cheek with your fingertips, ditto Her angelic shoulder, tantalising inner wrist, legendary earlobes, fabulous lips, etc. This is the time for a little Greek brandy, which, if mixed with pink champagne, makes a very Wicked Lady indeed.

And the mango?

Come on – use your imagination!

Best of luck!

Fiona Cooper was born in Bristol in 1955 and after many years working in London, she was defeated by parking meters and emigrated to Tyneside. Her novels include *Rotary Spokes*, *Heartbreak on the High Sierra*, *Not the Swiss Family Robinson*, *Jay Loves Lucy* and *The Empress of the Seven Oceans*. She has published a collection of stories, *I Believe in Angels*, and her work has been widely anthologised, including in *The Women's Press Book of New Myth and Magic* (The Women's Press, 1993).

Oh...Fudge! MARY DALY

The problem is: I do not cook. This is why I did not respond to the first gracious invitation to contribute to this volume. I was embarrassed, thinking of all those women with exotic recipes. Then came the inspiration: 'Oh, fudge!'

As I said, I do not cook — well, hardly. I mean, I can steam vegetables and bake potatoes, and I'm great at warming up gourmet take-out foods. As for recipes, I can recall (Re-Call) only two, which I acquired or invented at the age of ten. Only a few of my friends over the years have known about and actually tasted these delicacies — and then only after much begging and pleading on their part(s).

The first recipe is for chocolate fudge. This requires mixing intuitively measured amounts of cocoa, sugar, butter, salt, vanilla, and water, and boiling this bubbling mess at precisely the right temperature. Delicious! The second is for a dish known as 'Gashouse Egg'. This tasty treat is prepared as follows:

1. Put oil or butter in a frying pan.
2. Cut a large hole in a slice of bread and put this in pan.
3. Crack open an egg and drop this into the hole which is in the bread which is in the pan. Sprinkle salt on the egg.
4. Turn on the heat and fry until the bread is golden, spooning the oil or butter over the egg — and turning over in pan if desired.

While in the middle of writing this piece I phoned my friend Emily Culpepper who now lives in California – three thousand miles away from Boston. Emily had devoured my fudge twenty years ago. When I asked her if she had liked this concoction, she immediately Re-Called the experience and exclaimed: 'I *loved* it!' She then reminded me that she and the other members of the group gathered in my kitchen that evening (we called ourselves 'The Tigers') had pleaded repeatedly that I make it again. A certain Linda Barufaldi, who also now resides in California and who is noted for her oracular Barufaldian utterances, has reminded me that on that occasion she tasted the fudge and announced her verdict: 'Not only does she have a great mind. She can even cook!'

I now know that my Fudge is ineffable and immortal, evoking an experience that transcends time and space. Of course, great Fudge-making is never a solitary event. It requires a certain kind of environment in order to be so memorably savoured. Radical Lesbian Feminists' kitchens in the 1970s and 1980s were often such environments. They were centers for sharing fierce, sweet, Be-Laughing, Raging energy. In my kitchen the Fudge-cooking was accompanied by a Be-Witching chant. The words, which we shouted Out Loud, were:

Bubble, bubble
Toil and trouble
Fire burns and cauldrons bubble.
We Hex your empire to make it fall.
When you take on one of us you take on us all!

For a short while, some of that energy has been diffused. But it is Boiling inside many of us. Wild women are Volcanoes, getting ready to erupt again, more powerfully than ever. We are Brewing new brainstorms, Cooking up new ideas.

I have decided that very soon, on precisely the right night, a few women will be invited to my kitchen to stir up a batch of Be-Witching Fudge. I believe that such an event will help to fuel the new explosion of the women's revolution that must occur as we approach the turn of the millennium. According to certain proponents of quantum theory, one Quantum Leap can trigger simultaneous similar or identical events in other members of the same species – no matter how far the geographic distances that appear to separate them. So what if many groups of women 'just happen' to have similar Bubbling experiences in their kitchens when the Fudge-boiling starts up in my kitchen again?

Oh, about the Gashouse Egg recipe: It may not have such Ecstasy-evoking associations as the Fudge experience, but it certainly can sometimes stave off starvation while we conspire to overturn patriarchy. Try it with Irish breakfast tea and have a second serving.

Mary Daly describes herself as a Voyager; a Positively Revolting Hag, repelling the forces of patriarchy; and a Crafty Pirate, Righteously Plundering treasures of knowledge that have been stolen and hidden from women. She holds three doctorates including doctorates in theology and philosophy from the University of Fribourg, Switzerland. She is currently an associate professor of theology at Boston College where she teaches Feminist Ethics. Mary Daly is also the author of numerous books including *The Church and the Second Sex*, *Beyond God the Father*, *Gyn/Ecology*, *Pure Lust* and *Websters' First New Intergalactic Wickedary of the English Language*, Conjured in Cahoots with Jane Caputi as well as her work of autobiography, *Outercourse: The Be-Dazzling Voyage*.

Choristers' Cake SARA YEOMANS

This cake seems to contain most of my childhood and growing up in Gloucestershire, which is one reason that I love it. The other is that it is practically foolproof (the only time I failed with it was when I forgot to put the flour in).

My great-grandfather, my grandfather and my brother were all choristers at Gloucester Cathedral and so I am more earthed and deeply rooted in that building and that city and the hills that climb out of it than anywhere else. Mixing the cake reminds me of Evensongs, of listening to the boys' voices flying away into the fan vaulting and then of driving home up the hill to my grandmother's house to eat the Choristers' Cake and boiled eggs for tea.

My grandfather once took me up the stone stairs of the cathedral to the Whispering Gallery 'Stay there,' he said and disappeared. A long minute later his voice came clearly to me, whispering impossibly round the great curve of the gallery, where the accoustics are so perfect that even the tiniest sound reaches the listener without a dent or a blur across the whole width of the cathedral. All the way home to my grandmother's kitchen and the Choristers' Cake, I thought about the whisper and how it had travelled by magic along invisible lines to me.

Another time, after another Evensong, my grandfather introduced me to Robert of Normandy, who lay flat on his back on top of his tomb with his legs crossed and one toe pointing daintily in the air. 'When I was Top Boy here,' my grandfather said, 'we used to frighten visitors by pressing on his toe and making him sit up.' Robert of Normandy lies in a sort of metal cage now, to stop the choristers from terrifying visiting clerics. It's not nearly so much fun. We left him and drove back up the hill to the kitchen and the Choristers' Cake.

Now I boil the cake and turn down the gas and remember my grandmother's kitchen and the Aga with its drying rack slung on ropes above the hot plates and the smell of hot dust and ashes when she riddled the boiler.

It was a cake to eat after tobogganning. And before it. We kept the toboggan in the air-raid shelter we used as a den and we towed it along the lane, past the cemetery gates and up the steep pitch above the Chapel of Rest. The whole village stopped work when the real snow came and the buses didn't run so we couldn't get to school. We dragged our sledges and tin trays to the top of the pitch and hurtled crazily down, two hundred yards to the lane and the drystone wall at the bottom. The Vicar joined us once, flying down the pitch in his long black cassock, straight out of the cemetery after a funeral. They must have dug the grave before the snow fell, I thought. We tobogganned for hours until the white sky turned dusky and our fingers and feet turned numb. Then we went back to the kitchen for tea, boiled eggs and Choristers' Cake.

So I make this cake to pass on the things that I loved in my childhood and that I still carry inside me: the music and magic and mystery of Gloucester cathedral; the climb of the hills; the white space and speed and freedom of the snow; and the everlasting warmth and love and certainty of my grandmother's kitchen.

1 breakfast cup (75g/6oz) soft brown sugar	
450g/1lb mixed dried fruit, including peel	
115g/4oz butter	
1 tsp bicarbonate of soda (baking soda)	
2 large eggs	
½ cup/50g/2oz chopped nuts	
12 glacé (candied) cherries, cut in half	
a squeeze of lemon juice	
cinnamon and mixed spice	
2 teacups (1¾ cups/200g/7oz) self-raising flour	

Put the sugar, dried fruit, butter and bicarbonate of soda in a pan with 1 cup/250ml/8fl oz water. Simmer for 5 minutes. Leave to get cold. Then add the beaten eggs, nuts, cherries, lemon juice, spices and flour. Pour the mixture into an 18cm/7in tin which has been greased and lined. Bake in a preheated oven at 160°C/300°F or Gas Mark 2 for 2 hours.

Keep the cake in an airtight tin for at least a week before cutting.

Sara Yeomans was born in 1943 in Gloucestershire, and grew up there. She has worked as a teacher, scriptwriter and director, a freelance writer and journalist, and as an assistant editor on the magazine *Devon Life*. Her novel, *Travels with a Pram and Hot Flush and the Toy Boy* (1994) is published by The Women's Press.

Pie Diva (Brown Sugar Apple Spice Pie) DEVORAH MAJOR

When we get together, each part of the clan bringing a piece of the family feast, I am pies. Others switch dishes from gathering to gathering. One time they bring a main course and the next time a salad, or perhaps yams, or perhaps congo peas and rice, or perhaps a pot of greens, changing as they will with the season and temperament. But I am always pies. My niece once wrote an essay in school about my pies. When I come to a family event the question is not did I bring pies, but which flavors. Now in fact I cook a variety of dishes, and am actually quite capable in a kitchen. But family roles, both chosen and given, sometimes wrap themselves around you so comfortably that they simply become the way things are. Indeed my friend, who is more sister than friend, tells me that when I cross the country to visit her it is 'the law' that I make a pie. If I want to make a quiche, I may. If I choose to make some curried fish in coconut milk, it will be appreciated. But the pies, the pies are a requirement. I enjoy making pies. I accept my role, the pie diva of my family.

It started that summer when my grandparents crossed the continent to visit. My grandmother was a wonderful baker and provided a summer of desserts, something that was not a part of the California Major's regular menu. She made short cakes, and layer cakes, and all kinds of pies. While she would craft a flaky crust, I would peel apples, or measure sugar, or chatter idly. One day I went and picked wild blackberries from a neighbor's yard. I picked enough for one small tart. My grandmother handed me a piece of dough and taught me how to roll it out gently. Then I had to wash, pick, and sweeten the berries. Then add some spices. Everyone else had to wait until after dinner for dessert, but I had my tart before the big pie was even finished. It was delicious. I was determined to learn how to make tarts all by myself.

Although it was years before I learned how to make a crust, I quickly picked up on how to create exciting fillings. I also learned, standing at my grandmother's side, how a good pie dough felt. How light it should be, soft enough to roll out, but not too sticky. Strong enough to flip into a pie pan, but not too thick. I made it my mission to learn to make a crust that flaked like hers, where flavors of butter melted in your mouth, where the filling was secondary to the crust. The crust after all was the foundation of the pie, and everything stands or falls because of strong foundations. This is one recipe.

serves 6–8

THE CRUST

³/₄ cup/175g/6oz of very soft butter (vegetable shortening will do but it won't taste the same)

2 cups/225g/8oz all-purpose (plain) flour

2–6 tbsp cold water

The first thing to do when making a crust is relax. It isn't hard, it just has a bad reputation. The second thing is to handle it as little as possible.

Cut the butter into the flour. Use a pastry cutter if you have one and two knives if you don't. Take as long as it takes to make the flour look like cornmeal. It will be soft and fluffy. No flour should be completely dry. No butter should be visible. If you do this right the rest is a cinch.

Add 2 tbsp of the water to the flour mixture. Using a

96

fork, mix the water in until all is absorbed. If the crust mixture does not easily squeeze into a ball, it is too dry. Add more water, 1 tbsp at a time. If it is warm in your kitchen you tend to need less water. If it is cold you tend to need more. Once the crust mixture clings to the fork, roll it into two balls for the top and bottom crusts. If you refrigerate the dough for an hour, it will be easier to roll out. (I rarely do this because I don't plan my time that well.)

If you roll out the dough on lightly floured, waxed paper, you will be able to pick up the waxed paper and flip the crust into a 23cm/9in pie plate without breaking the crust. Try to roll the crust out only once! Remember to put flour under the crust ball and on top of it. Each time you roll you need to add more flour so the rolling pin won't stick. Each time you do, your crust gets heavier. Better a light crust that went into the pan in two pieces than a leaden crust that looks perfect, but tastes like cardboard.

Or – skip the crust and buy a pre-made crust. It won't be as good . . . but there's always the filling.

THE FILLING

$^{1}/_{2}$–$^{3}/_{4}$ cup/75–115g/3–4oz brown sugar (depends on sweetness of apples)
....
$^{1}/_{4}$ cup/25g/1oz all-purpose (plain) flour
....
1 tsp cinnamon
....
freshly grated nutmeg
....
a dash of cloves
....
6–8 large apples, peeled (optional), cored and sliced – I recommend having some tart variety apples and some sweet for a more interesting flavor
....
butter (optional)
....

Mix the sugar, flour and spices with apples. Put into the pie crust. Dot with butter if liked. Cover with the top crust on, and make a design in the crust to vent it.

Bake in a preheated oven at 200°C/400°F/Gas 6 for 1 hour or until the crust is lightly brown.

devorah major is a poet, fiction and essay writer, and novelist. The winner of the Black Caucus of the American Library Association's First Novelist Award, she is the author of *An Open Weave* (The Women's Press, 1996) and *street smarts* – her most recent book of poetry. She has an eighteen-year-old daughter, Yroko, and fifteen-year-old son, Iwa, who keep her creativity and energy flowing. Much of her inspiration in the kitchen draws from the teachings of her Jamaican grandmother, Ethel Allman Major. devorah major lives in San Francisco.

JANE RULE'S Brownies

Margaret Atwood comments: 'These are the brownies that Jane Rule doles out to the kids around her swimming pool on Galiano Island, B.C.'

2 cups/400g/14oz white sugar
....
4 squares/115g/4oz unsweetened chocolate
....
1/2 cup/115g/4oz butter
....
4 eggs
....
1/4 tsp salt
....
1 tsp vanilla extract
....
1 cup/115g/4oz all-purpose (plain) flour
....
1 cup/115g/4oz walnut pieces
....

Preheat the oven to 170°C/325°F/Gas 3. Sift the sugar and set aside. Over hot water, melt the chocolate and butter and set aside.

Beat the eggs until light and frothy, add the salt, then gradually add the sifted sugar. Fold the egg mixture into the melted chocolate and add the vanilla extract. Stir in the flour and combine well. Fold in the walnut pieces.

Bake in a greased 9 × 13in/23 × 33cm pan for 35 minutes. Cool, then cut into squares.

(From *The Canlit Foodbook* compiled and illustrated by Margaret Atwood, published by Collins, Toronto, 1987)

Jane Rule was born in Plainfield, New Jersey, in 1931 and

grew up in the Midwest and in California. In 1956 she moved to British Columbia where she now lives on Galiano Island. She has published numerous highly acclaimed novels, short stories and non-fiction, including *Desert of the Heart, Memory Board, This is Not for You* and *Against the Season.*

Traveller's Cold Tea Cake
EMMA DONOGHUE

I call this a traveller's cake because it has been such a comfort to me when I've been away from home. It has always reminded me of the 'elvish bread' in Tolkien's *Lord of the Rings*: endlessly pleasant and sustaining. Wrapped in a plastic bag or tin foil, this cake will stay moist and chewy forever. (Though, to be honest, I've never left it uneaten longer than a week.) If I'm staying in a hotel but feeling too cheap to pay for breakfast, I start each day with a thick slice of this cake: tea, fruit and comforting carbohydrate all in one.

The real time of trial, for any picky eater, is that first long trip away from home. When I was sixteen, I headed off to the Gaeltacht for the usual month-long course of Irish language, Irish dancing, and Irish mashed potato. My peers may have felt trepidation; I was in a blind panic. My only trust was in the bottom of my knapsack where a biscuit tin barricaded two huge rectangular tea cakes. Every evening I toyed with my repellently traditional dinner, then escaped to the bedroom, where I could munch tea cake while watching the Donegal sun begin its decline.

Eaters don't come much pickier than me; it is a social disability, and no doubt Freud would have a field day with my horror of 'goo'. Once, leaving the eight of us with a childminder for a week, my mother had to draw up a list of the things I could (rather than couldn't) eat: 'eggs, boiled, fried, but not scrambled', it began. Since then I have added to my list such intimidating delicacies as avocados and coffees. But at heart I suppose I remain a neurotic child who will always feel most comforted by a slab of fruit cake.

What I call a good recipe has to make my life simpler by being easily memorised, flexible in its ingredients, and tolerant of accidents. The Traveller's Cold Tea Cake is all-forgiving: I once went so far as to set it on fire, by letting its paper lining rest against the oven element, but it tasted fine in the end. Oh, and a good recipe should involve no more than five minutes of actual work in the kitchen: that's always been my idea of women's liberation.

2½ cups/375g/13oz mixed dried fruit (any proportion of sultanas (golden raisins), raisins, currants)
½ cup/115g/4oz sugar
1¼ cups/300ml/½ pt cold tea
2 eggs, beaten
1½ cups/175g/6oz plain (all-purpose) flour
1 level tsp baking powder
¼ tsp each of any number of the following: cinnamon, ginger, ground cloves, nutmeg
a generous scattering of poppy or caraway seeds (optional)

Soak the dried fruit and sugar overnight (or for at least 2 hours) in the cold tea. Stir in the eggs, flour, baking powder and spices. Spread in a lightly greased deep cake tin. Bake in a preheated oven at 190°C/375°F/Gas 5 for about 45 minutes, or until a knife comes out clean.

Born in Dublin, 1969, Emma Donoghue is a novelist (*Stir-Fry*, 1994 and *Hood*, 1995), playwright (*I Know My Own Heart*, 1993, and *Ladies & Gentlemen*, 1996), and historian (*Passions Between Women: British Lesbian Culture*

1668–1801, 1993). Her works have been translated into Dutch, German and Swedish. Donoghue's latest publication is an anthology of four centuries of women's love poetry, *What Sappho Would Have Said* (1996).

Dolly's Bread Pudding GILDA O'NEILL

Like so many working-class women, Polly, my grand-mother, born in the late 1880s, was a skilled magician in the kitchen; not in terms of her culinary refinements, but because she knew how to stretch a few ingredients into a meal that would satisfy her big, hungry family. A few bacon scraps and a sliced onion, wrapped in a thick roll of suet pastry, then boiled in a muslin cloth; a pound of sausages cut into pieces, and boiled with plenty of chopped onions in salted water, then thickened with flour and water paste just before serving with potatoes – just two of the many recipes passed on to Dolly, her daughter and my mother. Although they may lack sophistication, just the thought of sausage stew, bacon roll, or the bread pudding described below, takes me back to my childhood as surely as any Proustian pastry.

½ a stale loaf
....
3 tbsp sugar
....
1 teacup suet (vegetarian works fine)
....
½ teacup of raisins
....
½ teacup of currants
....
1 egg
....
½ box of mixed spice (about 2 well-heaped tbsp)
....

Note:

This was how the ingredients were listed for me, but the recipe is very flexible, and can be played around with to suit your taste. The working-class store cupboard was generally not very well – or reliably – stocked and recipes were adjusted to compensate. Peel might be added, for instance, or a little flour, which would alter the consistency, and although white bread was used traditionally, any bread will do.

Tear up the bread and soak in a basin of cold water, overnight if possible. Strain and squeeze dry. Beat the now very soft bread with a fork to get rid of any lumps. Add the remaining dry ingredients. Mix well, then moisten with the egg if it seems dry. Spread into a greased baking tin and cook in a moderate (180°C/350°F/Gas 4) oven until firm to the touch.

Serve hot or cold, in handful-sized slabs, with a cup of tea.

Gilda O'Neill was born and brought up in the East End of London in a traditional, working-class extended family. She dropped out of education when 15 years old and did a series of jobs and then married when 20 years old, having known John for just over a week. After the birth of her second child, Gilda returned to education as a mature student, taking a total of three university degrees including a Masters in Women's Studies. She has written six novels based in the East End, including her latest *Dream On* (1996) and has had two non-fiction works published by The Women's Press, *Pull No More Bines: Hop Picking – Memories of a Vanished Way of Life* (1990) and *A Night Out With the Girls: Women Having a Good Time* (1993). Her latest non-fiction project is a History of East London which Penguin has commissioned for publication in late 1998.

The Old, Old Hag's Chocolate Yeast Cake MEG O'BRIEN

This recipe came from my mother, who had gone completely gray and jokingly called herself 'the old, old hag' when she sent it to me, though she was probably only about fifty. I'd begged and pleaded for it for years, and she finally gave in, though she wrote at the top of it, 'Not to be given to anybody, and I mean anybody. Someday I am going to send it in to a contest and maybe win a prize.' My mother's been gone over twenty years now and I'm trusting she won't discover I've not only passed along her favorite, secret recipe, but published it. She always swore she'd come back to haunt me if I did.

Nothing would surprise me – not even my mother showing up in a ghostly mist to wag her finger at me after all these years. She was Irish, five-foot-two, as tough as she was soft, and funny as hell. My character Jesse, in my Jessica James series, is fashioned partly after her. So is Jesse's mother, Kate. My mother raised two children largely alone, working as a waitress to keep food on the table. I always knew when she was upset about something because all night long she would bake. She'd throw on an old housecoat, start with her chocolate yeast cake and just keep right on going till finally I'd wake up in the morning to find cake, pies and cookies all over the place. For my mother, who lived with an alcoholic husband, baking was therapy. My therapy was eating all those goodies – which I thankfully worked off every summer swimming, as we lived at the New Jersey shore.

The chocolate yeast cake was my favorite. My mother made it every year for my birthday, and often she'd wrap little charms in tissue paper and bake them right into it. I loved the surprise of finding them, but it was a challenge not to overlook one and break a tooth. She baked it for fellow workers, friends in her Bridge Club, for holidays, and for no particular reason at all except that everyone raved about it. The cake was dense, the icing thick and satisfying as fudge, and it went a long way. Instructions even went along with it: 'Don't cut in wedges. Cut thin, short, narrow slices. Make it *last*.'

When I took my mother's recipe out of its box the other day to write it down, it was so yellowed and tattered, I had to piece it together like a puzzle to make it out. Memories swept back in a flood, all of them good. I imagined I could smell the chocolate. I imagined I could see her dressed in that same old housecoat, her hair in short, brown, messed-up curls – blending, whipping, and mixing, then displaying her wares happily as the sun rose and I stumbled, smiling, into the kitchen, following my nose. That was the beauty in my mother's baking, and the true heritage she left me with. Not simply a recipe, or a cake, but the knowledge – by example – that no matter how bad things got, there was something about creating that reached deep into the soul, and for a little while, at least, made one whole.

1 cup/225g/8oz solid shortening, such as Crisco
2 cups/400g/14oz sugar
4 eggs, separated
½ yeast cake (15g/½oz fresh yeast)
¼ cup/60ml/2fl oz lukewarm water
3 squares/75g/3oz melted baking chocolate
2¾ cups/300g/11oz all-purpose (plain) flour
½ tsp salt
1 cup/250ml/8fl oz milk

1$\frac{1}{2}$ tsp baking soda (bicarbonate of soda)
....
2 tbsp boiling water
....
2 tsp vanilla extract
....

Cream the shortening with the sugar. Beat in the egg yolks, one at a time. Beat the egg whites separately and set aside. Add the yeast cake which has been softened and dissolved in the lukewarm water. Add the melted chocolate. Do not add while too hot. This spoils the yeast action.

Sift the flour with the salt. Add alternately to above mixture with the milk. Fold in the beaten egg whites. Cover the bowl with a dish towel (tea towel) and let sit overnight or about 5 or 6 hours.

Next morning, have three 9in/23cm layer cake pans greased and floured. Then dissolve the baking soda in the boiling water. Add to the cake mix all at once, with the vanilla, and beat. Don't be afraid to beat it. Pour into the cake pans. Tap the pans to eliminate the air bubbles in the batter. (Makes it denser.) Bake in a pre-heated oven at 180°C/350°F/Gas 4 for about 40 minutes or until done.

ICING:

Melt 3 squares/75g/3oz baking chocolate with 1 tbsp or more of Crisco. Add confectioner's (icing) sugar, 2 tsp vanilla, and about 1 tbsp of milk to make the desired consistency.

Meg O'Brien brought up five children and worked at a multitude of jobs from secretarial to housecleaning and freelance editing, become becoming a full-time writer. She is now the author of the bestselling Jessica 'Jesse' James mystery series: *Salmon in the Soup* (1993), *The Daphne Decisions* (1993), *Hare Today, Gone Tomorrow* (1993), *Eagles Die Too* (1993) and *A Bright Flamingo Shroud* (1996) – all published by The Women's Press.

Suburban Delight SARAH DREHER

My mother used to make this dessert back in the fifties. Instant foods – cake mixes, coffee, mashed potatoes – were all the rage. After the restrictions brought on by World War II, we wanted ease, indulgence and sugar. It was a particular favorite at bridge parties, on patios, at backyard barbecues, and as a 'side dish' for Christmas dinner.

In graduate school, I would make it for my roommates during times of stress, finals and all-nighters. It goes especially well with cramming. When I received my PhD, I invited my advisor to dinner and served it to her as a special treat. She thought it was terrible (she was from Vienna and constantly shocked by Americans). Our friendship survived.

During the seventies, it made a great accompaniment to chocolate bits, pizza, chips and dips, and other disgusting combinations of munchies. The varied textures were especially appreciated by those of us who consumed rec-reational, then-decriminalized, mind-altering substances.

It is still my dessert-of-choice, especially for those brunches that are so Politically Correct you could die. Goes great with tofu.

serves 4

| 1 cup/250ml/8fl oz can sweet Bing cherries |
| 1 cup/250ml/8fl oz boiling water |
| 1 box Cherry Jell-o (cherry jelly) |
| 1 cup/250ml/8 fl oz Dr Pepper, Coke, Pepsi, or other carbonated cola |

Drain the juice from the cherries. Add the boiling water to the Jell-o in a 1–quart/1l/1¾pt bowl. Stir until dissolved. Add the cola, stir. Chill until slightly set. Add the cherries, stir. Chill until firm.

Serve with whipped cream topping or 'as is'.

Note: If you want a particularly flavorful Jell-o, heat 1 cup/250ml/8fl oz of the cherry juice to boiling, substitute for the boiling water.

Sarah Dreher is the author of the bestselling Stoner McTavish mystery series which includes *Stoner McTavish* and *Bad Company* (The Women's Press, 1996). She is also a clinical psychologist and award-winning playwright. Sarah Dreher lives in Amherst, Massachusetts.

ALICE MUNRO'S Maple Mousse

Margaret Atwood comments: 'This is Alice Munro's own recipe, and she says it's really delicious.'

serves 6–8

1 tbsp gelatine

¹/₄ cup/60ml/2fl oz cold water

¹/₂ cup/125ml/4fl oz maple syrup

1 cup/250ml/8fl oz hot milk

¹/₄ cup/50g/2oz sugar

¹/₄ tsp salt

3 egg yolks, beaten

1 tbsp rum

1 cup/250ml/8fl oz whipped cream

Soak the gelatine in the cold water. Set aside.

Combine the maple syrup, hot milk, sugar, and salt in the top of a double boiler. Stir over hot water until the sugar is dissolved. Slowly pour a little of this syrup mixture over the beaten egg yolks and mix well. Add to the mixture in the double boiler, stirring well. Cook until it coats a wooden spoon heavily. Stir in the soaked gelatine and cook only until the gelatine dissolves.

Place in the refrigerator to cool, but do not let the gelatine set. Add the rum, fold in the whipped cream and pour into a mold or bowl. Chill for 12 hours before serving. Unmold the mousse and serve with extra maple syrup, if you want to be fancy.

(From *The Canlit Foodbook* compiled and illustrated by Margaret Atwood, published by Collins, Toronto, 1987).

Alice Munro was born in Wingham, Ontario, and went to the University of Western Ontario. In 1968 her first collection of stories, *Dance of the Happy Shades*, was published and won that year's Governor General's Award for Fiction. Her other works include *Something I've Been Meaning to Tell You*, *The Moons of Jupiter and Other Stories*, *Lives of Girls and Women*, and *The Beggar Maid*, which was nominated for the 1980 Booker Prize.

Figs Poached with Berries
DRUSILLA MODJESKA

I have the great advantage of living in Sydney, in Australia, a place which makes good cooks of us all. Or rather, in Sydney we have to work hard to ruin the ingredients we start with: the fish of the Pacific, the cornucopia of fruits from the tropical north, the varieties of potatoes and green vegetables – snake-beans to raddici – from the chilly south. Our cooking is a post-colonial blend of Thai, Mediterranean, and a dash of imagination. In this respect Australia's English heritage has been all but obliterated. The occasional roast is more likely to be served cold with a rocket salad or avocado salsa, then hot with gravy and Yorkshire pudding.

Sydney is the perfect place for someone like me who loves food but doesn't want to spend time on it. Or rather wants to spend the time eating (and talking), not cooking. So I've become the mistress of the stir-fry. It's fresh, it's quick, it's healthy, it's delicious. But it isn't exactly sexy. And just occasionally one wants to eat sexy. Which is when I remember my English heritage in its gaudiest form – D H Lawrence and Glenda Jackson – and think *figs*. In autumn in Sydney figs fall off the trees in back yards, people put out boxes of them on the street. The rest of the year they're a dollar a piece in smart fruit shops. But autumn's a good time for seduction, with the light slanting across the afternoon sky and the first edge of chill after months of too much heat. In these conditions I'll guarantee the effect of figs poached with berries. It's a recipe I got out of an Australian newspaper years ago and it turns up in different forms almost every year. It always uses berries: raspberries or blackberries, or those large red berries that are called red berries here but I think might be the same as loganberries or maybe youngberries in England. Any of these berries, in any combination, will do. (Do not use blueberries; for this recipe they are too blue.)

You will need a wide flattish saucepan into which you put a generous heap of berries, maybe a small punnet's worth, a little water (no more than a cup) and half a cup of sugar, more if you like sweet to be sweet. You boil this fairly vigorously until it turns into a thick, but not too thick, sweet sauce. A strip or two of lemon or orange peel will give it a tang, which I rather like. Or a very small strip of fresh lime peel. You can put this sauce through a sieve if you want it to be smooth, a proper purée; or you can leave it fruity. I'd recommend the purée even though it produces more washing up. I suppose it depends how serious the seduction is, and if you're prepared to risk one of those tiny seeds sticking between your teeth.

Meanwhile you will have prepared the figs by slitting them open, just a little, with a downward cross through the stem. While the purée is still quite runny, put the figs into the saucepan with their opened stems facing up, and simmer until they are soft, which doesn't take long – 5 minutes at the most. Take the figs out and reduce the purée, if it needs it, which it probably will, by boiling for a few more minutes until it takes on a thick enough consistency to fall from the spoon in a slow, elegant drip. Then let the figs and purée cool to room temperature.

The final task, hardly strenuous, is to make the figs look tempting on the plate, with the purée embellishing rather than drowning them. Add a few fresh berries, or some slivers of blanched almonds. Serve with a dab of good sheep's yoghurt or crème fraîche. I'll guarantee your success, at least on the aesthetics of this dish, for it comes out a glorious bruised reddish-purple colour.

Drusilla Modjeska was born in Britain in 1946 and has lived in Australia since 1971. She is the author of *Exiles at Home*, *Poppy* and *The Orchard* (The Women's Press, 1997) which won the Australian Booksellers Award two years in succession.

Nannie's Cornbread SUSAN STINSON

My grandmother's recipe for cornbread leaves me almost speechless. Nan Jordan was short and fat with wavy hair and the air of a beauty. She taught physical education at a Texas high school and drank diet soda out of Dixie cups. She said she didn't cook.

1½ cups/200g/7oz cornmeal
¾ cup/75g/3oz flour
1 tsp salt
2 tsp baking powder
2 tbsp shortening or bacon grease
1 egg
enough milk to make a thin batter

Heat the oven to 230°C/450°F/Gas 8. Put the grease into a 9in/23cm round cast-iron skillet, and place in the oven. Mix the dry ingredients in a big bowl. Add the egg and milk and stir until just blended.

Remove the skillet from the oven and carefully swirl the hot grease to coat the bottom and lower sides of the pan. Pour the remaining hot grease into the cornmeal mixture and stir lightly. Pour the batter into the hot skillet. Bake until the top browns, about 20–25 minutes.

Susan Stinson's fiction and poetry has appeared in numerous anthologies and magazines. She is the author of *Belly Songs: In Celebration of Fat Women*, as well as the novels *Fat Girl Dances with Rocks* and *Martha Moody* (The Women's Press, 1996). Susan Stinson was born in Amarillo, Texas, and now lives in Northampton, Massachusetts.

Atwood's Feed-Everyone Wheat Germ Muffins MARGARET ATWOOD

This recipe comes from my mother, and I make it frequently. The muffins store well, freeze and are better cold than hot ... perfect for breakfast, as you can make them ahead of time. A standby for hordes of people.

makes 3 or 4 dozen

3 eggs

1 cup/200g/7oz white sugar

1 cup/175g/6oz brown sugar

1 cup/250ml/8fl oz oil

3 cups/750ml/1¼pt buttermilk

3 cups/350g/12oz all-purpose (plain) flour

3 tsp baking soda (bicarbonate of soda)

3 tsp baking powder

3 cups/350g/12oz wheat germ

1 tsp salt

2 tsp vanilla extract

Preheat the oven to 200°C/400°F/Gas 6.

In a bowl mix together the eggs, white sugar, brown sugar, oil, and buttermilk.

In a second bowl, mix together the flour, baking soda, baking powder, wheat germ, and salt.

Pour the wet ingredients into the dry ingredients. Add the vanilla. Stir to blend, but do not overmix: if you wish, you may add 1 cup/175g/6oz of raisins, dates, or blueberries.

Fill muffin tins and bake for 20–25 minutes.

(From *The Canlit Foodbook* compiled and illustrated by Margaret Atwood, published by Collins, Toronto, 1987).

Margaret Atwood was born in Ottawa in 1939, and grew up in northern Quebec and Ontario, and in Toronto. She has lived in many other cities including Boston, Vancouver, Edmonton, Montreal, Berlin, Edinburgh and London, and has travelled extensively. Margaret Atwood has published over twenty books, including novels, poetry and literary criticism. Her latest is the novel, *Alias Grace*. She lives in Toronto with novelist Graham Gibson and their daughter Jess.

Soda Bread MOY McCRORY

Memories of food revolve around my sense of nationality, and of allegiance rather than any childhood recollection of meals lovingly prepared at home. My mother hated her kitchen and couldn't understand what all the fuss about vitamins was. Cooking was a duty, to be got through as quickly as possible so she fried everything and you ate fast so the plates could be put away. Although we often tried to suggest a healthier method, she would still say in her seventies that there wasn't time to use the grill. I'm not a cook, but I know that good food can be the easiest to prepare and my recipe is for soda bread which goes very well with those other Irish staples, fish and potatoes. These are the memories they bring . . .

Once, failing to peel a potato on a wretched camping holiday with an English family I was mocked mercilessly by the girl's father, 'Thinks she's Irish and can't even peel a spud!' He wouldn't let me claim I was English either, so I stood there, feeling the earth from the potato skin in my hand, wondering whose side I was allowed to be on. I was eight, and I've never been able to get that out of my mind. The source of his irritation was that my parents were Irish. My father was a Belfast man but a Catholic as was my mother.

Years later, I was a student in Belfast when the second, lesser, Unionist strike occurred. I had a room opposite the Ormeau Bakery. Every night at midnight, red lights and a siren came on as the Bakery's double doors lifted for the fleet of bread vans. The noise went on till two or three in the morning and I was so accustomed that I slept through it, until the first night of the strike when I woke at midnight, startled by silence. I lay there, a girl from Catholic stock, fearful in the solid Protestant quiet. Next morning, the small shops that dared open had day-old bread, then none. People had stocked their cupboards and I watched my milk sour.

In the summer of 1995, in those fragile days of an uneasy peace I went over to Ireland from England. We took a drive to Portavogie, a fishing village, to buy prawns. The road at the entrance to the village had been painted with a massive portrait of King Billy – this was Protestant, Unionist country. The portrait sported insignia: Loyal sons of Ulster, The Red Hand Brigade, No Surrender. As we drove under flapping red, white and blue I felt my skin greening until I was sure anyone looking would know I had come from alien territory. The unsettling silence of this peace was making everyone jumpy.

At the quay, the first boats were arriving. Two enormous grey seals waited in the dock. They were so familiar the fishermen had given them names. At the front a big, red man with hands like meat said he could sort us. We watched him weigh out langoustine into the EC recommended amounts. Then, over his shoulder, 'Do either of ye have a bag at all?' and he tipped the rest, well over a hundred, into a box we'd found.

'Will that do you now?' We were stunned. This Loyal Son of Ulster wouldn't take any money. 'Not at all,' he grinned, 'I've only given you the seals' share.' We could hear them barking from the bay.

'Listen to them boys, would you! You'll not be popular round here!' and he laughed, a big friendly laugh.

Seamus Carmichael's mother in Magherafelt gave me this recipe for soda bread. It's a makeshift version which omits buttermilk and soda flour, and uses approximations. It's bread, for difficult times, for sieges when the only milk sours, but especially as she said, for those of us in exile, in places where things aren't normally available.

4 cups/450g/1lb plain (all-purpose) flour
2½ cups/600ml/1pt sour milk
1 tsp bicarbonate of soda (baking soda)
pinch of salt

Sift dry ingredients together and rub the soda to get rid of lumps. Add the sour milk and work fast, as they begin to react immediately. Mix and turn as little as possible until you have an impossibly runny dough. Scoop this up and set it down on a well floured board. Turn it once. This provides the dough with a shell of flour which makes the next stage possible which is to lift and drop it on to a hot, unoiled griddle.

The way to test a griddle is to throw flour on it and watch it brown. It ought to take a minute. Any longer, it's not hot enough. For those without griddles, a heavy-bottomed frying pan works just as well.

As the dough lurches terrifyingly, you can reshape it into a neat round once it's over the heat. Turn this bread once only to cook both sides.

The way to test if soda bread is cooked through is to press the top down; if it goes down easily and rises back, it's cooked.

Soda bread is good with both sweet and savoury accompaniments. A favourite meal of mine combines the bread with grilled or barbecued prawns, and baked potatoes. Soda can be made fancy with sugar, sultanas and nuts. You can try colouring it green for 17 March (St Patrick's Day), or orange for 12 July (Battle of the Boyne). Unlike people, bread has yet to take sides.

Moy McCrory is the author of three collections of short stories and a novel, *The Fading Shrine*. She has also contributed to numerous anthologies including *The Plot Against Mary: More Seasonal Stories* (The Women's Press, 1992).

Home-Baked Whole Wheat Bread
ROBIN MORGAN

'All poems are made by one poet, a woman poet'
—Marina Tsvetaeva

Learning as if for the first time how
to make poetry.
No additives, no processed flours:
only whole grains, salt, honey, yeast.
I have kneaded shadows
and watched them rise, swallowed them,
fed them to others, too long,
fighting to cheat starvation.

> When the last rat was devoured
> in the refugee camp of Rashidiyeh,
> the men petitioned the mullahs
> for religious dispensation
> to permit the eating of human flesh.
> No one asked who would cook it.

> The already unclean ones whose lives
> were dumb clay, they
> would cook it, know how
> to spice it, disguise it,
> lie as they served it,
> so as not to disgust sons, fathers,
> brothers, and husbands: the raw flesh
> they had birthed, suckled,
> cooked, and still fed.

Still trying to learn
how to make sense of it,
where is the boiling point,
what degree heat melts the crystal,
at what precise moment
the nerves sing recognition.

A lifetime spent learning
how to spice it, disguise it, lie
as I serve it: this dumb clay, this raw flesh
that is me.

> Men make impressions, arbitrary decisions, names
> for themselves, wars, profits, laws, reputations,
> deals, fortunes, threats, enemies, promises, tracks.

> Women make do, ends meet, babies, way, clothing,
> breakfast and dinner and supper, quilts, homes,
> apologies, baskets, beds, light of it, room.

Beginning again, unlearning how
to make jokes, compromises and bargains,
the best of it. Relearning how
to make trouble, a living, a practice of politics.
Cracking wheat, crushing millet, dissolving
salt crystals, pounding the dough. Waiting
the first rise. Reshaping the dough. Waiting
the second. Heating the oven of metal or clay . . .

Over and over, practicing how
to make a fresh start, making the most of knowing
the worst of it – not what's assumed:
that they can torture, degrade, kill, erase you,
but this – that they can just tire you out.
My son, grown now, sits making
his music, pressing all the right keys,

his darkening hair tarnished by late summer light.
He is the last man
I will forgive.
Again, every woman surveying
the state of her life as again it withers away,
searching the ashes for something, finding
an edge of it, tugging, trying to free
the shredded banner of her red worker heart.

    Marion Todd, of Fairbury, Nebraska, was shy.
    She never thought of breaking the law.
    'One day,' she said, 'I was suddenly hit
    with an image of a nuclear train being blocked
    by a pile of wheat – a grain that sustains life.'
    So, holding a handful of wheat, she sat down
    on the tracks and waited for hours in February
    snow,
    until the train carrying nuclear missiles
    bore down on her, until it finally
    screamed to a stop two feet away, until
    they called the police, until she was dragged
    off, charged, and jailed – still shy.

Again and again learning how
to make peace:
cracking open the whole grain of anger,
crushing the fear, dissolving the sense
of futility, deliberately making
believe,
pounding, shaping, reshaping the act –
arbitrary but this time our own.
One woman demands *bread and roses*. Another invokes
bread, blood, poetry. In Chile, the women say bread
is the face of God. Feeding each other
the honey and salt of it, learning to make
the connections.

Clay is the wild crystal
making itself through eons of weathering
by the pounding, cracking, crushing of rocks,
the dissolving of rocks, the absorption
of water in minuscule pores, developing 'defects'
in crystalline lattices which collect energy, store it,
transmit it. This is one definition
of a life form.

A regular crystal is perfect, blank until
it receives an imposed pattern of charges.
                    But clay replicates, layering
pattern on pattern of ions coded in flaws.
Disorder, the woman scientist whispers,
is precisely the thing which can hold information.
Strike an ordinary lump of clay with a hammer:
it blows ultraviolet energy for a month.

Learning as if for the first time how
to make merry:
woman to woman, eye to wide open eye –
a choice arbitrary
as my own will, my flesh undisguised,
no longer young but no longer helpless.
Rare only in how I express this, our shared
commonality, I am wild clay
whose nerves sing recognition, blow energy, store
information, transmit these messages
in willful, flawed code
to a woman, a sister, a lover
who rises like yeast, like a poem, raw
in my hand, teaching me now
as if for the first time how
to make love.

I want to make
this so plain
that every woman can feed herself with it,
make it her own, make it
mean what she chooses, make
demands of it, make
it available, make
mischief, a difference, a miracle, ready.
I want to say this in the quietest voice possible:

*Give us this day
our arbitrary bread.*

Do I make myself
clear?

2 tbsp active dry yeast
¼ cup/75g/3oz honey
1 tbsp sea salt
3 cups/750ml/1¼pt hot water
7–8 cups/795g/1¾lb whole wheat flour
olive oil
butter/margarine for pan-greasing

Whisk the yeast, honey, salt, and hot water in a large bowl to dissolve thoroughly. Add the first 4 cups/450g/1lb of flour in two equal portions, mixing each well before continuing. Add another 1 cup/115g/4oz of flour and work in. Spread 1 cup/115g/4oz of flour on a marble slab or wood kneading board. Scrape the batter onto the board and knead in the flour. Add another ¹/₂ cup/50g/2oz of flour and knead in. Add as much of the remaining flour as necessary to keep the dough from sticking to your hand, and for good substance and cohesion (if you hold up the dough ball, palm down, and it stays cohesive, that's good).

When sufficient flour is worked in, knead the dough meditatively for 15–20 minutes, or energetically for 10 minutes. Don't be afraid to sprinkle more flour as necessary to keep the dough from sticking to your hands or the board. You can't overknead, so if you're unsure, keep going. Very faint wrinkles will begin to appear on the dough's surface when it's ready. Drizzle a few drops of olive oil into the mixing bowl, drop in the dough ball, and turn it around to oil it on all sides.

Wet a clean dish towel (tea towel) with hot water, wring out, and cover the bowl; place it in a warm draft-free place to rise. The first rise should take about an hour; it may take more. You can test its readiness by sticking your finger into it and watching the dough's reaction: if the hole slowly fills itself in, then the dough isn't risen enough.

Dump the risen dough back onto your lightly floured surface, 'punch' it down to get out the air pockets, and knead lightly for a few minutes. Then divide the dough into three equal parts. Grease three bread pans of about 9 inches by 5 inches/23cm by 12cm (you can use disposable ones but wash and recycle them over and over). Shape the loaves by flattening the dough; roll into loaf shape, and tuck in the ends; make sure the 'seam' is on the bottom. Fit the loaves into the pans, cover them with the rewetted towel, and set in a warm spot for the second rise – which should take about half the time of the first. The loaves will rise to or even above the level of the pans by the time they're ready to bake.

Bake in a preheated moderate (180–190°C/350–375°F/Gas 4–5) oven for about 40 minutes (if a wooden skewer inserted into the loaves comes out dry and clean, they're done). If the bread is not cooked but the crust seems on the verge of scorching, turn off the oven but leave the loaves in for 10 minutes. Cool slightly but eat while warm.

VARIANTS:

You can add raisins, chopped nuts or chives, or grated orange peel at the first kneading stage. You can also substitute wheat germ, millet, rye flour, or muesli for the fifth cup of flour, for a rich, hearty texture. You can also freeze these loaves for later thawing and warming. Once familiar with the basic approach, experiment with additions or combinations. Enjoy your own creativity, the zen-like bliss of patient kneading, and the fact that, while the loaves are baking, the whole house smells like god Herself.

Robin Morgan, an award-winning poet, novelist, political theorist and feminist activist, has published fourteen books including the now classic anthologies, *Sisterhood is Powerful* and *Sisterhood is Global*. Her writing has been translated into nine languages. Recent books include *The Demon Lover, The Anatomy of Freedom, The Word of a Woman* and *The Mer-Child: A Legend for Children and Other Adults*. She lives in New York City.

INDEX

The Women's Press is Britain's leading women's publishing house. Established in 1978, we publish high-quality fiction and non-fiction from outstanding women writers worldwide. Our exciting and diverse list includes literary fiction, detective novels, biography and autobiography, health, women's studies, handbooks, literary criticism, psychology and self help, the arts, our popular Livewire Books series for young women and the bestselling annual *Women Artists Diary* featuring beautiful colour and black-and-white illustrations from the best in contemporary women's art.

If you would like more information about our books or about our mail order book club, please send an A5 sae for our latest catalogue and complete list to:

The Sales Department
The Women's Press Ltd
34 Great Sutton Street
London EC1V 0DX
Tel: 0171 251 3007
Fax: 0171 608 1938